Everybody Has a Body

Everybody Has a Body
Science from Head to Toe

Activities Book for Teachers of Children Ages 3–6

By
Robert E. Rockwell
Robert A. Williams
Elizabeth A. Sherwood

Illustrated by
Laurel J. Sweetman

gryphon house
Mt. Rainier, Maryland

© 1992 Robert E. Rockwell, Robert A. Williams and Elizabeth A. Sherwood
Published by Gryphon House, Inc., 3706 Otis Street, Mt. Rainier, MD 20712
ISBN: 0-87659-158-6
Library of Congress Catalog Number: 92–53890

Design: Graves, Fowler & Associates
Cover Photo: ©1992 Burwell & Burwell

Publisher's Cataloging in Publication
(Prepared by Quality Books Inc.)

Rockwell, Robert E.
    Everybody has a body : science from head to toe / Robert E. Rockwell,
Robert A. Williams, Elizabeth A. Sherwood.
    p. cm.
    Includes index.
    ISBN 0-87659-158-6
    1. Body, Human--Study and teaching (Preschool). 2. Health--Study
and teaching (Preschool). 3. Education, Preschool--Activity programs.
I. Williams, Robert A. II. Sherwood, Elizabeth A. III. Title. IV. Title:
Science from head to toe.

LB1140.4.H4R6 1992   372'.37'049
                                 QBI92-803

This book is dedicated to
our faith, love, and trust
in each other
and
to family and friends
who have supported us through
our ten years of working together

... Kathryn, Amanda, Robert, Teri ~ Tom, Terry, Kate, Hal & Charly ~ Aunt Betty ~ JoAnn & Wally ~ Shannon ~ Claudia ~ Michael, ... Donna, Susan & Janet ~ Erma Lee ~ Bill, Jennifer & Will ~ Katie & Clarence, Jeff & Blanca, Sissy & Shawn ...

Bob ◁ Bob
Elizabeth

Special Thanks To:
Kathy Charner, editor extraordinaire
Laurel Sweetman, for joining us on yet another venture
Dr. Susan Miener, who read our book for accurate medical content
The Gryphon & his Minions, who have supported us through the years
Don Malone, whose remarkable skill & compassion allowed this book's completion

TABLE OF CONTENTS

Chapter Three—Here's Looking at You: How Eyes See

Chapter Four—Listen Up: A World of Sounds

Chapter Five—Your Nose Knows: It's More Than a Smeller Teller

Chapter Six—Open Wide and Say "Ahh": A Look Inside Your Mouth

FOREWORD

Children are natural-born scientists. They come into this life as infants using the natural scientific tools of smell, taste, sight, hearing, and touch to explore, interact, and learn about the magnificent world that they have entered. One of the first environments that they encounter is their own body. As time passes they will acquire knowledge about themselves. This knowledge can be intertwined with pre-science skills, health information, literature, self-concept development, and body awareness.

As we prepared this book, we felt that many readers might see it as a health book. It is that, but even more, it is a science book—a science book that uses our own natural laboratory, the body. We want children to be curious, to be eager to find possible answers to the why, what, when, and how. We want them to be aware of their uniqueness and to accept differences, to know that being different doesn't mean being better or worse. As teachers of young children, it is your responsibility to insure that no one be embarrassed or made to have negative feelings about their bodies. Everybody has a body, and that body is the greatest!

The age appropriateness given for each activity is an approximation, and is based upon our observations of many children who have tried them. Remember, each child has a particular background of experience that will guide any responses to an activity. The children and their reactions should be the final judges of whether the activity is appropriate for them or not.

Young Children and Scientific Discovery

Scientific discovery needs to be an integral part of every early childhood curriculum. Young children must make discoveries so that they begin to understand how their world is put together. At this early stage in life, children have a natural curiosity—an intrinsic need to know and understand. Early childhood educators can recognize and utilize this period of heightened motivation to learn and children need to seek information outside of themselves. Proper discovery activities can promote children's self-esteem, develop their problem-solving skills, and enhance their language acquisition.

When young children are engaged in scientific discovery, they learn, through trial and error, that they can have an effect on the world. They learn that their actions have consequences, sometimes positive and sometimes negative, but always as a result of their own power and decisions. The more young children are given the opportunity to frequently engage in decision making, the more systematic their decisions become. As a result, they come to understand that their thoughts and actions are important, therefore increasing their awareness and self-esteem.

The act of scientific discovery involves children's mastery of several science process skills. Observation, the most basic of these skills, heightens a child's sense of awareness. Through focused observations, children begin to understand the structure and order of their surroundings. They build a base of information that can be used at any time to explain phenomena. As they move from an egocentric view of the world to a more exocentric one, they will have a better understanding of their role in their environment. This understanding of place serves to build a sense of compassion for other living things in their world.

Once children have learned to make careful and concise observations of relevant information, the next step is to help them attach meaning to their observations. Two of the science process skills that enable them to find this meaning are inference and prediction. Children use inferences to explain their observations: Why did the water run out of the overturned glass? What will a magnet pick up? The answers to these questions, generated by the actual experiences, are inferences. If they couple the observations with their logical inferences as a basis for making guesses about future events, they are predicting.

The greatest outcome scientific discovery provides young children is the enhancement and development of language through stimulating experiences. As children are afforded the opportunity to interact with a variety of science-related activities and materials, they are simultaneously exposed to the vocabulary that accompanies them. When young children manipulate, watch, listen, smell, and taste their way through the discoveries, they begin to internalize the accompanying labels. This provides them with the language they need to both think about and describe their experiences.

Dr. David Winnett
Assistant Professor—Science Education
Southern Illinois University at Edwardsville

Sharon Winnett
Director Pre-Kindergarten Program
Hillsboro, Illinois

The Whole Child or Integral "I": Self-Concept and the Development of the New Scientist

Central to the well-being of everybody is a knowledge and understanding of the self—the "Who am I?" and "How do I feel about who I am?"; these are questions we all ask. How fitting that in a science book dedicated to taking a close look at the body and how it functions, the authors realize the need to look at the whole child, not just its parts.

Through this affirmation of the whole child, they are acknowledging the interrelatedness and interconnectedness of our body's parts and systems—one to another. Indeed, each part or system has unique aspects that merit closer scrutiny to develop a better understanding of each use and function. But only through use of this knowledge can we begin to fully comprehend and appreciate how one part or system relies on another to perform its function. Although independent, they do not operate in isolation; they are a part of an integrated whole.

If we break a bone in an arm or leg, we are able to get along without the full use of the function of that limb by compensating in various ways. We learn to write with the "wrong arm" or how to use crutches, because we know the cast will come off before too long. In the same vein, modern science and medicine have worked closely together to make great strides in creating artificial parts to approximate and imitate the functions of many body parts when the "real thing" will no longer do. But what happens when we break, we injure, we hurt a part of our body on which a cast cannot be put? Will that person be relegated to living a "fractured" life forever? What happens when there is no prosthesis to compensate? Will permanent damage result?

In *The Caprice Immensity* Gwen Frostig states, "Fragmented parts are inexplicable—only through integration can the entirety be manifested." Our heart provides the life-sustaining pump that feeds and nourishes our body; it is essential to our physical well-being. At the same time, the "heart" is also essential to the emotional well-being of every body. For, at the "heart" of every child is the "I"; the all that I am.

Both "hearts" are integral to our body; we cannot live without our "hearts." Take time to listen to the "heart" of every child.

Eloise R. Hayman
Early Childhood Consultant
The Purple Squirrel, Inc.

Self-Esteem, the Disabled, and
Discovery Science: Natural Processes

Educators and other professionals spend an inordinate amount of time explaining what children with disabilities cannot do when, in fact, they should be measuring and articulating what they see as the child's assets and abilities. The negative atmosphere created by these expectations has a detrimental effect upon the child and upon everyone who has contact with that child. It should be no surprise that children with disabilities often approach learning tasks with an apprehension that has its roots in prior negative experiences, both educational and social. If no one thinks they can do a task, then no one will encourage them, and sure enough, they do not perform.

How do we begin to reverse this trend? The answer may be more simple than we think. The earlier a disability is diagnosed, the better. The more rapidly we can begin a positive early intervention program, the more everyone will benefit. Rappaport (1966) compared the development of a handicapped and a normal child:

> The latter achieves developmental milestones as anticipated by parents and perceives their pleasure and pride, rejoices in his or her own accomplishments, and develops the attitude that "I am one who can." In marked contrast, a child with a handicap is delayed in development and perceives the tension, fear, and possible rejection by anxious parents. Knowing failure, he or she thinks "I am one who cannot." Self-concept, positive or negative, affects all areas of functioning—academic, social, and psychological.

It is critical that we provide disabled children with early, positive, interactive learning experiences. The activities within this book allow for the discovery of the world around the child. Discovery by itself is a positive process; however, it is greatly enhanced by the interaction of the child with those "significant others" in his life: parents, teachers, and friends. Learning occurs, positive feelings develop, the child feels secure in attempting new things, and the cloud of apprehension toward new experiences begins to dissolve. As self-confidence grows, self-esteem is enhanced. Parents need to realize that the earlier they recognize the existence of a disability, the earlier they will begin their travel toward acceptance of the child. Over the last two decades, research has indicated that there is a great deal to be gained by early intervention, both educationally and socially, for children with disabilities. Bricker (1986) brought forth three basic reasons for intervention at the earliest possible point. First, early learning has always served as a foundation for later education. The earlier you begin, the more likely will be the child's later ability to master more complex skills. Second is the matter of family support. The child, parents, and siblings will get support that can prevent the development of other problems. For example, a child with a learning disability can develop a behavioral problem because of lack of understanding and support. Lastly, through counseling and medical and financial assistance, a family can get the services they need to adjust to the disabled child and provide a psychologically nurturing environment.

Early intervention should not be perceived as the only thing we need to do to assist the disabled to develop a positive self-concept. It is, however, the one point we need not argue about. The creation of a positive learning environment in the early years makes it a lot easier for the child to enter the public school system. Attempting to undo five or six years of feelings that "I cannot" is extremely difficult.

The science activities found in this book will not guarantee that a disabled child will be a success in later life, but they will enhance the child's chances. Disabled children, through participation with "significant others," begin to discover the world around them. The activities develop feelings of success and accomplishment. The basic discoveries are usually concrete in nature, but as time goes by and exposure and confidence build, the children begin to see the complexities and relationships between things in their world. The ability to think abstractly is increased, and they are able to transfer what they learn from one situation to another. As an aside, often the retarded are able to master addition, subtraction, and some degree of multiplication, but never understand how these skills are used to survive in the community. They cannot make the transfer from the classroom to the outside world because they have no experience in that process. The discovery method is one way to assist the child to develop the wider view and transfer the skills from where they are learned to where they are used.

Research has shown that the learning process is the same in all individuals. What separates individuals is the rate of learning. None of the activities in this book need to be altered for a learning disabled or retarded child. Obviously, there may be a need to make adaptations to accommodate physical disabilities. You must also remember that more time may be needed for the concept to be fully understood. This should not discourage you in working with children, but only make you more aware of their individual learning rates. Studies by Ellis in the last ten years have shown that the retarded, once they have learned and mastered a concept, can remember and use that information as well as non-retarded individuals. The key is still learning, feeling good about what is learned, and a positive sense of self.

Too many disabled spend the majority of their lives before, during, and after the school year feeling as if they are nobody. Positive early intervention and continuous support will enhance these disabled individuals' self-concept, and perhaps allow them to state, as does Rev. Jesse Jackson, "I am somebody."

Robert M. Wagner
Professor Special Education
Southern Illinois University at Edwardsville

Emerging Literacy and Science: Natural Processes

Joshua and Michelle are huddled in the corner of their classroom busily discussing whether their hands and feet can pick up any of the items in the basket—a marble, a pencil, blocks, a basketball, a baseball. They group their predictions on the rug. Ms. Parker, their teacher, provides a large piece of newsprint and magic markers for them and asks them to record their predictions. After experimenting with each item with their hands and feet, they record the results on the same chart with encouragement from Ms. Parker. After the chart is complete, Joshua and Michelle make a list of the words related to their work on another piece of newsprint. This list is hung on the wall in the corner where Joshua and Michelle were working. The next day Ms. Parker asks the class to recall the experience the previous day and takes dictation as they verbally sequence the process, the predictions, and the results.

This scenario in an early childhood classroom reflects the natural relationship between science and language. Joshua, Michelle, and Ms. Parker were implementing "Fantastic Feats with Feet." In so doing, children, with guidance from an adult, purposefully manipulate concrete objects while naturally using the four basic components of language: speaking, listening, reading, and writing. Literacy in young children naturally emerges as they interact with each other and with the environment.

Emerging literacy is being promoted through the efforts of Marie Clay in New Zealand, Kenneth Goodman in the United States, and Frank Smith in the United States and Canada. Theoretically, literacy emerges not in a systematic, sequential manner but rather in response to the printed language and social environment (Hall, 1987). The concept of "emergent" suggests development from within the child. This notion is consistent with Developmentally Appropriate Practice as promoted by the National Association for the Education of Young Children (Bredekamp, 1987).

The idea of encouraging children's literacy as it emerges has encouraged teachers to think of reading and writing as processes that begin long before first grade. The goal is not to teach children to read, rather it is to make literacy interesting, functional, and meaningful (Schickedanz, 1986). Teachers often think of science and language as discrete curricular areas in an early childhood program. However, as children actively participate in science experiences, a skilled early childhood teacher will facilitate literacy experiences that are related and, therefore, meaningful.

The classroom environment needs to reflect support for the relationship between literacy and science. Science areas in the room need to have picture books related to topics being addressed and reference materials such as science dictionaries. The writing center in the classroom needs to include items conducive to recording and writing about science. These items include file folders, index cards, and Post-it notes as well as a variety of writing tools and paper.

As young children express their thoughts on paper, the stages of writing become evident. Science is the ideal medium through which symbols take on meaning. As children experiment with magnets or explore objects that sink and float in water, they record their predictions and results. A teacher who supports child-initiated learning will encourage children to invent their own symbols in recording predictions and results. Marie Clay (1975) identified thirteen concepts involved in emergent writing. The concepts emphasize the importance of accepting children's attempts as the valuable first stages of writing development.

The early childhood classroom that actively supports emerging literacy as related to science will have print materials that are related to the children's experiences abounding. The experiences may be both teacher-directed and child-initiated. Specific literacy strategies include word lists, charts, graphs, commercial pictures, labels, signs, stories read by the teacher, books written and dictated by children, and sequence charts.

This relationship between emerging literacy and science is natural —just as young children's curiosity and self-expression is natural.

Susan W. Nall
Professor Early Childhood Education
Southern Illinois University at Edwardsville

Where Do Health and Nutrition Fit?

The years of early childhood provide the optimum time to promote good health and nutrition practices. This is the time when teachers of young children can begin to emphasize an awareness of environmental and social issues that will have a lasting impact upon the child's well-being. Early childhood programs provide the perfect setting in which to give children correct information and to help them establish good habits and attitudes about their bodies and themselves (Endres and Rockwell, 1990). Such learning becomes much more meaningful when integrated throughout the daily curriculum. For example, exercise can accompany music, nutrition can be stressed during snack or science, and hand washing can be combined with cooking and art. By utilizing this integrative approach, we can help children begin to understand the value of the concepts of good health and nutrition. It is critical that teachers and parents set and model good examples of health and nutrition practices. By serving as role models, we will help create an environment in which children learn, understand, and begin to assume responsibility for their own well-being.

Personal Safety: An Issue In Teaching Body Awareness

We have developed a series of activities that use the children's own bodies to teach scientific concepts and skills. As the teaching proceeds, we are sure that many opportunities will arise to teach in areas other than science. An area that concerns everyone is personal safety education. The topic is sure to surface in a series of activities in which the children's bodies are vehicles for learning. Therefore, it would be natural to consider including personal safety lessons right then. This is not a book on personal safety education for children, but we do feel that training in this area is a necessary part of every early childhood curriculum. Many such curriculum guides exist. If you do not have one readily available, call your local college, your curriculum director, area social services agency, police department, or Rape Crisis Center for help. Personal safety education is important because all of us care about children. Preschoolers are especially vulnerable because of their lack of experience and knowledge. In addition, their trusting nature and small size can put them in positions in which their safety may be jeopardized. Providing children with safe alternatives in potentially dangerous situations is desirable rather than the development of fears and anxiety over possible problems. Personal safety education should include fire, water, and street safety as well as information to protect the children from sexual and physical abuse. Sharing this information with children does not in any way lessen the responsibility of adults to ensure children's safety. It is merely an additional safeguard. It tells children that they and their bodies are important to protect. It also lets them know that adults will help them whenever necessary. A safe and healthy body is more important than any facts we may teach.

Declaration of the Rights of the Child (from The United Nations)

Every child in the world has rights!
1. Every child has the right to be strong and healthy in mind and body.
2. Every child has the right to have a name and a country.
3. Every child has the right to have enough food to eat, a place to live, and a doctor's care.
4. Every child who is handicapped has the right to special treatment and care.
5. Every child has the right to grow up in a family feeling safe, loved, and understood.
6. Every child has the right to go to school and to play.
7. Every child has the right to be protected from cruelty or unfair treatment.
8. Every child has the right to grow up without fear and hatred, and with love, peace, and friendship all around.

Children are wonderful gifts. As with all gifts, there is responsibility involved in keeping that gift safe and at its best. Parents, and all adults, are accountable and must be sure that a child's freedoms and privileges are always respected. While we are telling children how grateful we are for their many, many special ways, we also need to consider the rights of children. These rights are obvious and should be given without any conditions!!!

Parent Involvement

Parents, as the child's first care givers and teachers, have both the right and the responsibility to be involved in their child's formal education. The early childhood program has both the responsibility and the need to involve parents in their children's learning. It has never been possible for the school to help children grow and develop without mutual respect and support between the home and the school. Today in early childhood programming, this cooperation between the home and school emerges as an even more powerful force in children's achievement. Research has clearly shown that parental involvement is a critical variable in a child's education. Results of studies conducted in a variety of educational and care settings over the past twenty-five years suggest that parents who helped their children by establishing a strong learning environment in the home, who stimulated their children's interest in learning, and who supported their children's natural curiosity, fostered attitudes that were important to their children's achievement in school. The involvement of parents was also found to influence the child's later school achievement. In addition, parents who were involved with the school developed more positive attitudes toward the school and its goals.

Early childhood programs must not only welcome parents but actively encourage and seek their participation in the education of their children. Teachers and administrators must have the skill and desire to involve all families in meaningful roles within the school community. Parents of different cultural, ethnic, and familial backgrounds must perceive the school as their school. It is important that the parents' first experience with the school be a positive one. Careful planning and understanding on the part of program directors and teachers in particular is needed to:

1. recognize and value the role of the parent as the first teacher of the child;
2. respect the parents as the persons who know their children best;
3. accept the cultural and familial uniqueness of each family;
4. create an environment in which all parents feel welcome and capable of contributing to their children's education; and
5. recognize that there are a variety of ways parents may choose to be involved.

As teachers we are faced with the problem of scientific illiteracy on the part of the general population. How can we expect parents to be involved when most of them have little or no background in science themselves? The challenge is to present experiences in which parents, children, and teachers can work together as partners as they acquire scientific knowledge and skills. The activities in this book lend themselves nicely to both individual and collaborative explanation. As we have conducted workshops for parents and children, the enthusiasm and the natural curiosity of the children has been observed in the adults as well. This has been especially true when we elaborated on the meaning of hands-on interaction with the environment. The Chinese proverb—I Hear and I Forget, I See and I Remember, I Do and I Understand—rings true.

Resources and Helpers

The Yellow Pages:

Ear

Acoustical Consultants
Audiologists
Deaf Instruments
Hearing Aids
Otorhinolaryngology
Physicians
Sound Amplification

Nose

Allergist
Odor Control
Otolaryngology
Otorhinolaryngology
Respirator/therapy

Hands and Feet

Chiropodist
Manicuring
Podiatrist

Eye

Artificial Eyes
Blind Libraries
Ophthalmologist
Optical Goods
Optician Oculist
Optometrist

Mouth

Clinics, dental
Dentists
Orthodontist

Arms and Legs

Chiropractic
Dancing Schools
Orthopedic
Osteopathic

Physical Therapy
Reflexologist

Internal Organs

Cardiology
Cardiovascular
Endocrinology
Gastroenterology
Gynecology
Hematology
Neurology
Obstetrics
Pulmonary
Thoracic
Urology

Miscellaneous

Barber
Blood Banks
Child Abuse Information
Cosmetologist
Dermatologists
Infectious Diseases
Nurses
Nutritionist
Naturopath
Pediatrician
Skin Care

Organizations

Eye

American Academy of Ophthalmology
655 Beach Street
San Francisco, CA 94109

American Foundation for the Blind
15 West 16th Street
New York, NY 10011

American Optometric Association
243 Lindberg Blvd.
St. Louis, MO 63141

National Society to Prevent Blindness
500 East Remington Road
Schaumburg, IL 60173

Mental Health

National Mental Health Association
1021 Prince Street
Alexandria, Virginia 22314-2971

Feet and Hands

American Podiatric Medical Association
9312 Old Georgetown Road
Bethesda, Maryland 20814

Ear

American Speech-Language-Hearing
  Association
10801 Rockville Pike
Rockville, Maryland 20852

Child Abuse

American Academy of Child and
  Adolescent Psychiatry
3615 Wisconsin Avenue, NW
Washington, DC 20016

American Professional Society on the
  Abuse of Children
University of Chicago
School of Social Service Administration
969 East 60th Street
Chicago, IL 60637

Childhelp USA
National Headquarters
Woodland Hills, CA 91370

Parental Stress Services
600 South Federal Suite 205
Chicago, IL 60605

Special Organizations

American Academy of Pediatrics
141 Northwest Blvd, PO Box 927
Elk Grove Village, IL 60009-0927

American Association for Hearing and
  Speech Action
18801 Rockville Place
Rockville, MD 20852

American College of Radiology
1891 Preston White Drive
Reston, VA 22091

American Heart Association
7320 Greenville Avenue
Dallas, TX 75231

American Medical Association
515 North State Street
Chicago, IL 60610

The American Occupational Therapy
  Association
1383 Piccard Drive, Suite 301
Rockville, MD 20850-4375

Asthma and Allergy Foundation of
  America
1717 Massachusetts Ave. NW, Suite 305
Washington, D.C. 20036

National Association for the Education
  of Young Children
1834 Connecticut Avenue, NW
Washington, DC 20009-5786

National Dairy Council
6300 North River Road
Rosemont, IL 60018-4233

National Easter Seal Society
70 East Lake Street
Chicago, IL 60601

National Safety Council
444 North Michigan Avenue
Chicago, IL 60611

Voices in Action, Inc.
PO Box 148309
Chicago, IL 60614

How to Use This Book

This book is organized in much the same way as our three previous publications, *Hug a Tree*, *Mudpies to Magnets*, and *More Mudpies to Magnets*. Each chapter begins with *"Information Please,"* a collection of facts and background information related to the chapter topic. This gives the teacher a good base of information quickly and easily. Nursery rhymes, poetry, thoughts, ideas, and interesting bits of information are interspersed throughout the book. We hope this will give you inspiration to add your own thoughts. You will also find art work created by some of the three to six year old children who have enjoyed many of these activities. As you will see, even very young children can indicate their observations through drawings.

Within each chapter, the activities are grouped by body part or function. For example, in the chapter on the mouth, the activities exploring taste are grouped together. The age appropriateness for each activity is an approximation, and is based on observations of many children who tried them. Remember, all children have individual histories of experiences that will influence their responses to these activities. Your observations and knowledge of the children should be the key factors in determining whether an activity is appropriate or not.

Each activity is introduced with a brief descriptive paragraph. *"Language you can use"* lists words and ideas for encouraging children to talk about experiences, ask questions, and describe what they are thinking. This process will serve to clarify or confirm their observations as they interact with the materials and with each other.

"Things you will need" lists everything you will need to conduct the activity. Most of the items are things you will have on hand or can be easily found at a grocery or hardware store. Some items, as well as additional information, can be obtained from the resources people and organizations listed in Resources and Helpers in the introductory section.

"What to do" provides a step-by-step guide to the activity. Remember as you work with the children that you are a facilitator and participant, not the person with the right answers. The children need to explore, interact, and seek answers for themselves. Do not hesitate to modify or adapt the directions to meet the needs of your children.

"Want to do more?" gives ideas to expand the activity. The ideas are designed to build upon the foundation of the original experience. Many of the activities and their extensions are appropriate for older children. This is especially useful when working with the broad age range of children often found in school-aged childcare programs or other groups with a wide range of experiences. All the children can be participating at their own level.

Developmentally Appropriate Practices

In *Developmentally Appropriate Practice in Early Childhood Programs Serving Children from Birth Through Age 8**, The National Association for the Education of Young Children (NAEYC), emphasizes that there should be a suitable match between the capabilities and interests of children and the expectations of the curriculum and teaching methods. The content of the guidelines was strongly influenced by developmental and educational theories and research findings that emphasize direct experience, adult warmth, concrete materials, child-initiated activity, and social interaction. Grouped under categories such as curriculum goals, teaching strategies, and cognitive development, each statement of an appropriate practice is provided with a corresponding inappropriate practice. For example, the following pair is found within the category of "cognitive development" in programs for 4 and 5 year old children.

Appropriate practice—Children develop understanding of concepts about themselves, others, and the world around them through observation, interacting with people and real objects, and seeking solutions to concrete problems. Learning about math, science, social studies, health, and other content areas are all integrated through meaningful activities such as building with blocks; measuring sand, water or ingredients for cooking; observing changes in the environment; working with wood and tools; sorting objects for a purpose; exploring animals, plants, water, wheels, and gears; singing and listening to music from various cultures; and drawing, painting, and working with clay. Routines help children keep themselves healthy and safe.

Inappropriate Practice—Instruction stresses isolated skill development through memorization and rote learning, such as counting, circling an item on a work sheet, memorizing facts, watching demonstrations, drilling with flash cards, or looking at maps. Children's cognitive development is seen as fragmented in content areas such as math, science, or social studies, and times are set aside to concentrate on each area.

The guidelines are intended to be useful to teachers, administrators, parents, policy makers, and others involved in programs serving children from birth to age 8 in schools, centers and homes.

* To obtain a copy of *Developmentally Appropriate Practice in Early Childhood Programs Serving Children from Birth through Age 8,* write to: NAEYC, 1834 Connecticut Ave. NW, Washington, D.C. 20009-5786.

References

Bredekamp, S. (Ed.), (1987). *Developmentally Appropriate Practice in Early Childhood Programs Serving Children from Birth to Age 8*. Washington, DC: National Association for the Education of Young Children.

Bricker, D.D. (1986) "An analysis of early intervention programs: Attendant issues and future direction." In R.J. Morris (Ed). *Special Education: Research and Trends* (pp 28-65). New York: Pergamon Press.

Clay, M. (1975). *What Did I Write?* Portsmouth: Heinmann.

Ellis, N.R. (1970) "Memory processes in retardates and normals." In N.R. Ellis (Ed). *International Review of Research in Mental Retardation* (Vol 4) New York: Academic Press.

Endres, J. and Rockwell, R. (1990). *Food, Nutrition, and the Young Child*. Columbus, OH: Merrill Publishing Company

Frostig, G. (1983) *The Caprice Immensity*. Benzonia, Michigan: Presscraft Papers, Inc.

Hall, N. (1987). *The Emergence of Literacy*. Portsmouth: Heinmann.

Rappaport, S.R. (1966) "Personality factors teachers need for relationship structure." In W. M. Cruickshank (Ed). *The Teacher of Brain Injured Children: A Discussion of the Bases for Competency* (pp 49-55). Syracuse, NY: Syracuse University Press.

Schickedanz, J. (1986). *More Than ABC's*. Washington, DC: National Association for the Education of Young Children.

Smith, Frank. (1985). *Reading Without Nonsense*. New York: Teachers College.

Keeping in Touch: Using Your Hands and Feet

Keeping in Touch:
Using Your Hands and Feet

INFORMATION PLEASE

The hands and feet of each of us serve several very important but very different jobs. Both the hands and the feet are parts of the SKELETAL system. The skeletal system gives the human body its shape, without bones everyone would collapse into a pile. The skeletal system works in conjunction with the MUSCULAR system to allow the body to move. The fleshy part of the hands and feet are the muscles; the hard parts are bones. Muscles are attached to bones by special tissues called TENDONS. The places where bones come together are JOINTS. The bones in the joints are held together by LIGAMENTS. CARTILAGE is a soft material found at the end of bones and serves as a pad or cushion.

When a child is born, 270 bones make up the skeleton. As the child grows, some of these bones fuse together so that an adult will have only 206 bones. Through growth in the bones, a child will become taller. When a child is born the bones are soft, consisting mostly of cartilage; they harden into the skeleton from the center out. Growth will take place at the soft ends of the bones. When the bones harden a child has reached the final growth or height. Hands and feet of children and adults come in all different sizes, and are composed of many tiny bones. In fact, almost half of the total body bones (106) are found in the hands, wrists, feet, and ankles.

How do hands work?

The many bones are necessary for the intricate movements and support needed by the body. Both the hands and the feet are almost devoid of muscles. Tendons come down from the arms and are attached to the bones, functioning to move the bones found there. We use our hands to grab hold of and pick up objects. Hands are also used to touch and feel things. Our hands contain four types of nerve endings that make the fingers and thumbs very sensitive. Hands help us to feel heat, cold, pressure, and pain. Blind persons use their sense of touch when reading the raised print of BRAILLE.

What bones are in the hand?

The hand consists of the WRIST, PALM, BACK, four FINGERS, and THUMB. Twenty-six bones make up this skeletal structure. The CARPEL bones form the wrist, the METACARPAL bones form the palm and back, while the PHALANGES are the bones of the fingers. The extremely flexible hands are so very important to our everyday lives and work.

How do feet work?

We use our feet for very different purposes than the hands. The primary functions of the feet are to support and hold the body in the upright position and to support the body in walking. The flexibility of feet is less than hands, even though the foot has the same 26 bones that are found in the hand.

What bones are in the foot?

The foot consists of the ANKLE, HEEL, SOLE, ARCH, TOP, and five TOES. The TARSAL bones form the ankle, the METATARSAL bones make up the area of the sole, arch, heel and top, while the PHALANGES are the toes. The foot bones are much larger and more cumbersome because their job is to carry and support the body, not move, grab, or feel as in the hands.

When we look at the hands or the feet, however, we do not see the bones or the muscles that give them strength and flexibility. What we see is the SKIN. The skin forms the cover over the muscle and skeletal assembly, protecting the tissue under it by keeping foreign substances out. At the same time, heat and liquids are kept inside the body. The skin is a very specialized layer called the EPIDERMIS. On the hands and feet, the skin has distinctive designs we use to identify people. The prints made of the designs are never lost and always remain the same throughout life. FINGERNAILS and TOENAILS are special structures of the skin. HAIR is also a collection of skin cells. The only place on the body that nails are found are the hands and feet, while one of the few places that hair does not grow is on the palms of the hands and the soles of the feet.

Odd Socks

Odd socks—everyone has them. How about using odd socks to explore classification?

What to do

1. This activity is to be done by a small group of children. Give the group 10-15 socks.
2. What is one way we can sort the socks into piles? The children will offer many suggestions such as color, size, or fabric. Have the children group the socks by a chosen attribute.
3. Classify the socks by a variety of attributes.
4. Have the children group the socks by size; this can be done by placing all socks of similar size in piles.
5. Another way we can classify by size is to put objects in order, from smallest to largest. Socks of the same size may be stacked on top of each other in a pile.
6. Ask the children who can wear each sock in the stack. Which one can they wear? Notice that as we grow our feet change in size.

Want to do more?

Measure the socks, draw pictures of socks on feet. Fill the socks with paper to get a three-dimensional effect. Compare sock size to shoe size.

Language you can use

match
classify
sort
group
attribute
smallest
largest

Things you will need

all the odd socks that the children can collect, including adult and baby socks

Tickle Touch

Language you can use

tickle
touch
skin
tactile
sensation

Things you will need

feathers

paper and
marker to record
results

The skin is the major receptor of tactile sensation. We all enjoy the fun and laughter that comes from a good tickle. The tickle is the result of a soft touch to a very sensitive part of our body. This activity uses an object to determine which is the most sensitive to the touch of a feather, the foot or the hand.

What to do

1. The children remove their shoes and socks; then are grouped in pairs.
2. One child extends both hands and feet.
3. The other child, the tickler, predicts which body part—the foot or the hand—is the most ticklish.
4. The first child agrees or disagrees.
5. The tickler proceeds to tickle the foot and the palm of the hand with a light stroke of a feather.
6. Was the tickler right or wrong with the prediction?

Want to do more?

Tickle the ears, under the nose, the arm, stomach, etc.

Wet Socks, Dry Socks

"Don't go out with wet socks, you will catch a cold!" Sound familiar!? "Get out of those wet clothes, you will freeze." Well, there is some scientific sense to those pieces of advice. Evaporation describes the change water makes as it moves from a liquid to a gas. In changing states, energy or heat is required, causing a cooling. You can keep cool on a hot day, or be too cool on a cold day. Allowing the children to experience evaporation can help them to make sound decisions about wearing wet clothes—maybe.

What to do

1. Discuss evaporation with the children. Demonstrate evaporation by wetting the blackboard with a paper towel, then allowing it to dry.
2. When water disappears into the air, this process is called evaporation. When evaporation occurs, cooling takes place. That is why you should change socks or clothing when they become wet. Let's see how it feels when you have wet socks by conducting a simple experiment.
3. Give each child a matched pair of socks. Put them both on, then wet each left sock. A squirt bottle works well for this. Now walk around the room. Chanting, "Left is wet, right is dry. Which one is cool? Can you tell why?" will add some pizazz to the walk.
4. Discuss which foot is cooler. (Tape right foot/left footprints on the floor in front of a fan to accentuate the cooling.)
5. Have the children, one at a time, stand correctly on the footprints and tell which foot is colder, right or left, which foot is wet.
6. Make a chart of which foot is colder, left or right, wet or dry.

Want to do more?

Try the same experiment using hands. Change materials; woolen socks are able to hold heat better.

Language you can use

evaporation
wet
dry
cooling
colder
fan
right
left

Things you will need

pair of socks for each child

water
paper towel
squirt bottle
fan

right and left footprints taped on floor

paper and marker to record observations

All Different Kinds of Feet

Language you can use

compare
feet
prints
toes
heels
size
measure

Things you will need

pictures of animals such as opossum, squirrel, fox, deer, raccoon, and rabbit

pictures of front and back footprints of the animals (see illustrations)

Feet come in all sizes and shapes. Footprints are just as unique and different as fingerprints. It's hard to examine the foot of a woodland animal since most of them are shy, secretive, and nocturnal, but you can be sure they are around by the footprints (tracks) that they leave behind. This activity lets us examine the footprints of some common woodland mammals and compare them to our own. What is the same? What is different?

What to do

1. Let children observe the illustrations of mammals, their feet, and their footprints. How are their feet like ours? What is the same? What is different?
2. Make a comparison list for each mammal foot to a human foot, i.e., heels, toes, toenails, size.

Want to do more?

Which feet climb trees best? Which feet swim best? Which feet run the fastest? Examine insect feet. Which animals have no feet? How do they move? Examine the footprints of a dog, cat, or guinea pig.

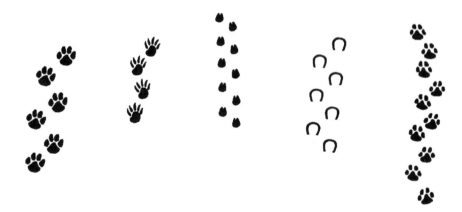

A Zoo Full of Feet

Look closely at everyone's feet. Draw attention to all the characteristics. Draw feet. Get to know feet. Now let's look at feet from the rest of the animal world. Do you want to look at front or hind feet? You choose. But remember that some front feet in animals are adapted to serve as hands.

What to do

1. The children must be made aware of their own feet and the things they can do. They need to have explored them in detail to be able to compare animals' appendages to their own feet.
2. While at the zoo, farm, or pet store, as each animal is observed, talk about how the feet look and how the animal uses them. How would the children do a similar task?
3. As the children are discussing the actions and their comparisons, an adult should note the comments on paper for review after the trip.
4. During lunch or at a rest time during the trip, talk about the animals' feet and how the animals used them. As each is reviewed, ask the children to act out the animal movements. Talk about the similarities and differences between various animal feet and their own feet.

Want to do more?

Take a video camera along and record the movement of each animal. Then take another video of kids doing imitations of the animal movements. Ask them to remember which animal's movement they were making.

Feet, Feet down the street
Jump, jump over a bump
Hop, hop, hop on top
Skip, skip, never trip
How many ways can your feet move?
As many ways you can choose.

Curry the Donkey

Language you can use

different
feet
toes
claws
nails
footpads
modified
animal names

Things you will need

a trip to the zoo, farm, or pet store

paper and pen

Fantastic Feats With Feet

Language you can use

pick
hold
dexterity

Things you will need

paper and marker to record predictions

variety of materials from very large to marble size such as a marble, pencil, blocks, basketball, baseball

Hands and feet have evolved differently over the millions of years that humans have been on the planet. The feet have accepted less and less use in the daily activities of people as hands pick up, hold, and manipulate objects. The feet can be trained to do such tasks, but not easily, because they are formed differently.

What to do

1. Place five objects in the center of the floor.
2. Ask children to predict whether they can pick up an object with their hands, feet, both, or neither.
3. Record the predictions on a chart.
4. Try picking up each object, first with hands, then with feet.
5. Compare the results to the predictions. Some objects are too big to be picked up by one hand or one foot and require using two hands or two feet.

Want to do more?

Try other objects. What shapes are easy to pick up with feet? Try to develop a rule that will describe what can be picked up by hands or feet. Is left or right handed/footed easier?

This little pig went to market.
This little pig stayed home.
This little pig had roast beef.
This little pig had none.
And this little pig cried,
"Wee, wee, wee," all the way home.

Make Your Own X-ray

Some of the children or a member of their family will very likely have been to the doctor for a broken bone. Take advantage of that expensive, unfortunate situation. With an X-ray in hand and a hand in the finger paint, you can develop your own pretend X-rays to teach children that bones really do exist under the skin and flesh of our bodies.

What to do

1. Trace each child's hands. Place names at the top of each page.
2. Can you tell which is the right or left hand? How do you know?
3. Discuss how our body is held into place by a skeleton made of bones. We cannot see the bones, but we can feel them. Bones allow us to hold our hands rigid and to move them to pick up things. We cannot see bones unless we use a special X-ray machine. Have any of you had an X-ray taken?
4. Look at the X-ray. See how the bones of the hands show in the X-ray.
5. Now make pretend X-rays by putting the proper hand in finger paint and placing it on top of the hand drawing (make sure the hand is well covered with paint).
6. Hang the X-rays on the wall.

Want to do more?

Have children bring in X-rays from their doctors. Make clay models of the bones as they appear under the skin.

Language you can use

bones
feet
hands
skeleton

Things you will need

X-rays of feet and hands

paper and crayons, finger paint

Helping Hands

Language you can use

helpers
helping
jobs
tasks
ourselves
others
people
pretend
share
take turns

This activity lets children use their imaginations as they imitate the various tasks that their hands do to help themselves and others.

What to do

1. Let's think of things that helping hands can do, for example, push, pull, cut, hammer, hold, carry, polish, shake, lift, comb, tie.
2. Play a pretend game. Let children take turns demonstrating how their hands help by doing hand movements.
3. The other children attempt to guess the tasks the hands are doing.
4. Do a tally sheet of the things helping hands do at home, at school, on the playground, at grandma and grandpa's house, for ourselves, for others.

Things you will need

hands

paper and marker for tally sheet

Want to do more?

How do other members of our families use their helping hands? Show the children various items such as a hammer, a paintbrush, or a toothbrush and have them pretend to use the item.

How Many Hands Tall?

Ever wonder how tall a horse is? Horse breeders use a part of their body to measure their horses. That part of the body is the hand. The horse is measured from the ground to the highest point of the withers (the ridge between the shoulder bones). A hand equals 10 centimeters (4"). A horse that stands 14.2 hands is 1.5 meters (58") high. Most ponies are less than 14.2 hands. Most race horses are 15 to 16.2 hands high. Some draft horses are 20 hands high. That's big! If a hand equals 10 centimeters, how many hands high are you?

What to do

1. Have a child stand against the wall. Let the children estimate how many hands tall the child is.
3. An adult then measures the child, hand by hand, beginning at the ground and going up to the top of the head as the children count.
4. How accurate were the predictions? Do they become more accurate with practice?
5. How do we compare in size to horses?

Want to do more?

Do the same activity, but help the children do body tracings on butcher paper. Let them measure themselves with their own hands. Cut out paper hands and use them to measure. What happens when you measure the same things with a child's hand, then an adult's hand?

Language you can use

hands
measure
inches
foot
meters
centimeters
tall
measurement

Things you will need

Shadow Pictures

Language you can use

animals
shadows
look
listen
identify
noise
sounds

Things you will need

white sheet for a screen

a light to shine on it, or a clear section of wall that is bright with light and catches the silhouette

Children love to use their fingers and hands to make shadow pictures. Close observation is needed to learn the hand position required to make a specific shadow picture. We can also use our ears if the shadow picture maker uses sounds that help us to identify them.

What to do

1. Set up the screen.
2. Ask the children if they can make shadow pictures with their hands, placing their hands between the light and the screen to cast a shadow.
3. Let them take turns showing their shadow pictures—complete with sound effects.
4. Have the other children attempt to identify the various shadow pictures.
5. Encourage them to imitate each other's pictures and create new ones.

Want to do more?

Develop a short story about the shadow pictures. Do a shadow play. Find a book on shadow play and add it to your repertoire. Make some shadow puppets. Make shadow shapes from clay, collage material, or anything else that works.

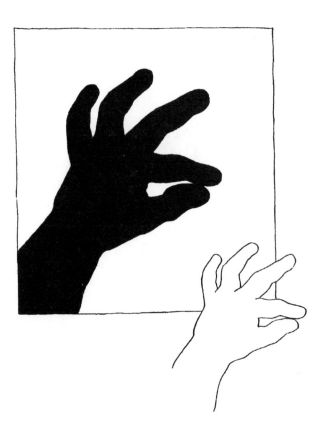

A Round of Applause

We use our hands by clapping them together to make a noise when we want to show others that we like what they have done. When we clap, it is called applause. We applaud a baby's first steps, first words, just about every first there is. We applaud others as we grow older. It makes people feel good. Encourage and participate with your children as they applaud their appreciation for an occurrence in the classroom, on a field trip, or on the playground. This activity lets you clap for one of the most important persons—yourself!

What to do

1. At circle time, ask the children to think about something they did that made them feel good. Give some examples of your own. Spotlight a few people each day, including the adults in the classroom. We all do helpful and special things.
2. After a person states an accomplishment, the group gives her a round of applause.
3. After some people have shared an accomplishment and been applauded, close the activity by stating, "Let's give ourselves a round of applause." Make a circle in the air with your clapping hands.

Want to do more?

Have the children applaud in various shapes such as a triangle, a square. Bring in other people who help with your program, such as an administrator, custodian, or cook and applaud their contributions.

Language you can use

applause
applaud
clap
proud
good

Things you will need

hands

See Through Hands

Language you can use

wrist
palm
fingers
thumb
ankle
heel
sole
arch
toes

Technical terms are listed in IN-FORMATION PLEASE at the beginning of this chapter

Do you remember discovering as a child that you could shine a flashlight through your hand? While this discovery doesn't qualify as one of life's thrilling milestones, it's still pretty interesting! It also provides a means of exploring the structure of the hand. Besides, children love messing around with flashlights.

What to do

1. Show children pictures of hands. Point out and let them name the parts—wrist, palm, fingers, thumb.
2. Share the X-ray—explaining that this is what it looks like inside the hand. See the many bones. The bones have names. Name and point out the bones on the X-ray.
3. Darken the room. Place a flashlight in the palm of the child's hand. Turn it on. What parts can you see? What parts can't you see?
4. Have children trace their hands on drawing paper.
5. Label the parts of the hand.

Want to do more?

Have children measure their hands on the drawings. Let them take them home and have the parents and other family members trace their hands on the same sheet of drawing paper. Compare the size and shape of the hands of the family members. Repeat the entire activity with feet.

Things you will need

X-rays of hands
pictures of hands
drawing paper
powerful flashlight
crayons

Feet in a Bag

The nervous system makes it possible for the human body to have many sensations. Different sensory nerves located in special sense organs send nerve impulses (messages to the brain), and the brain recognizes the impulses as sensations. This activity explores the sensation of touch. The sense organ that is involved is the skin on the hands and the skin on the feet. By using the sense of touch, the children compare which is the most sensitive, the hands or the feet.

What to do

1. Let the children see the objects before they are placed in the bag. Do not let them touch the objects.
2. Put the objects in the bag and mix them up.
3. Put a blindfold on one child.
4. Ask the children to predict which body part (the foot or the hand) will be able to most easily identify the objects in the bag, using only the sensation of touch.
5. Have the child stick a foot into the bag.
6. The child identifies one object, then pulls it out of the bag with the toes.
7. Keep a tally sheet for correct responses and number of tries. After an attempt has been made to identify all of the objects using the foot, switch to the hand and follow the same procedure.

Want to do more?

Choose other objects to test the hand and feet sensitivity of hard-soft, hot-cold, smooth-rough.

Language you can use

touch
feel
sensation
hands
feet
skin

Talk about the sense organs of the body—the skin, the nose, the eye, and the ear as well as their various sensations; for example, touch, pressure, heat, cold, pain, smell, taste, sight, heavy, and balance

Things you will need

an assortment of eight to ten objects—marbles, nuts, rocks, shells

blindfold
mystery bag
paper and marker

Frozen Fingers

Language you can use

finger
splint
flexible
stiff
bend

Things you will need

tape, popsicle sticks

small objects to pick up—some easy and some difficult

at least one large item

An important attribute of human fingers is their dexterity. Children know that they can pick up very small objects. Yet, unless they are handicapped in the use of their hands, they have little realization of how important that natural ability to flex, bend, and manipulate their fingers is to everyday life. Let's do a bit of manipulation of those digits and see how picking up things will progress.

What to do

1. Talk about how we are able to pick up things with our fingers. Note how fingers are able to fit around objects, both large and small.
2. Place the objects in front of a child. The child picks up each object as its name is called out. Was the object easy or hard to lift?
3. Cut popsicle sticks to the length of the first two fingers and tape in place (see illustration).
4. Try picking up the same objects. What happens now that the child has "frozen fingers"?
5. Discuss how important healthy, agile fingers are to our everyday experiences. Talk about the fact that some people have hands that don't work as well as most hands do. What are some things they do to compensate? The children may have their own experiences to share—a grandparent with arthritis, a sister with cerebral palsy, or their own broken finger.

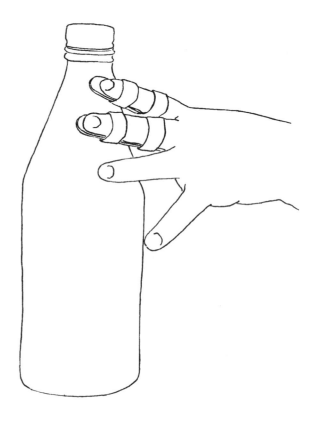

Want to do more?

See "Thumbs Up" in *More Mudpies to Magnets.* "Freeze" different fingers. Arrange a visit with someone who has a disability affecting the hands, either through an accident or disease. Be sure the person is comfortable with small children and sharing the techniques that have allowed for independence.

Picture Perfect Palm Prints

Each of us has hands that are different from each other and are different from other people's hands. As children develop observational skills by matching the hand pairs made during this activity, they will discover how each hand varies. The difference is especially evident when comparing left and right hands. Our hands are not symmetrical, are they?

What to do

1. Help the children make a pair of hand prints on one piece of paper. Be sure to put the children's names on the underside of the paper.
2. Have some of the children make a pair of the tops of hand prints or make two sets of hand prints, one of the tops of the hands and one of the palms.
3. Allow the prints to dry, then cut them apart.
4. Place the children in groups of two or three. Mix the group's hand sets.
5. Have the children match the hand pairs.
6. Check the pairs by matching the names on the backs.

Want to do more?

Use different colors for right and left hands. Increase the mix and match group size to increase difficulty. Take photographs of hands and mix and match. Experiment with fingerprints.

Language you can use

left
right
match
pair
symmetrical

Things you will need

finger paints paper and marker

Pair Roundup

Language you can use

match
texture
rough
smooth
hard
soft
sharp
shape words
pair
pass

Things you will need

sets of textures, such as two pieces of sandpaper, two pieces of cotton, two hard plastic squares, etc.

What is a section on fingers and toes without a touch activity? The object of this game is to find two textures that match and describe them. Pull together a pile of pairs and get into the feel of things.

What to do

1. Show the children the sets of objects. Explain that two of each texture are in each set. Pass the objects around one at a time for the children to feel. As the objects are circulated, ask the children to use descriptive words about each object.
2. When the children are familiar with the objects and the descriptions, sit in a circle and give each child one of a pair.
3. Ask the children to close their eyes and begin to pass the matching objects around the circle behind their backs. If they feel the match for their object, they open their eyes to check. If they are right, they place the matching pair in their laps. The children continue to pass the objects around the circle until all the pairs are found.

Want to do more?

Use hot and cold objects. Use shapes. Add odd feeling items such as "stickery," sticky, yucky, and so forth. Can the children name the items without looking at them?

Mystery Bead Bags

Macaroni, blocks, beads, shells, and other various odds and ends that we teachers collect can be used to teach science process skills. This activity teaches patterns and ordering as well as creative art and an appreciation for the sensitivity of touch that our fingers bring to the fascinating world about us.

What to do

1. The teacher prepares a bead pattern, placing beads on a string in a certain pattern.
2. The teacher also prepares mystery bead bags. In these bags are beads that will match the teacher's bead pattern.
3. Each child is given a mystery bead bag and a bead string.
4. Instruct the children to reach in the mystery bead bag and to find by touch (no peeking) the beads that match the teacher's bead pattern.
5. The children attempt to copy the teacher's bead pattern using only the sense of touch.

Want to do more?

For less experienced children, have them simply find matching pairs. Do the same activity with blocks and other objects, i.e., macaroni shapes. Let children make their own pattern to be copied by others.

Language you can use

shape names
pattern
order
mystery
bead
bag
touch
fingers

Things you will need

collection of large beads (or shells, blocks, macaroni) of various shapes and textures

paper or cloth bags
yarn or string

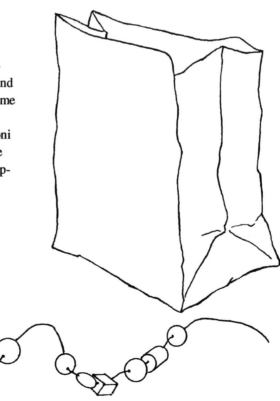

Helping Our Fingers: Play

Language you can use

fingers
hands
pointer
ring
middle
small
thumb
people
five

Things you will need

hands and fingers

Children enjoy using their fingers as they participate in action rhymes and finger plays. Finger play provides the first steps of the necessary stages of random manipulations that lead to concrete thinking. These finger plays introduce the children to specific fingers on their hands. Visit any early childhood classroom and you'll learn many more!

What to do

1. The teacher tells the children, "Hold your hands up. Watch my hand(s) and listen and move your fingers the same way I do."
2. The teacher then says a finger rhyme with children following his or her lead.

> *There is a little mouse hiding in a hole*
> *(hand closed with thumb inside)*
> *It will come out if we talk soft and low*
> *Open up a window, another and another*
> *(raise little finger, then next, then next)*
> *There is the mouse hiding in the covers*
> *(thumb under index finger)*

Want to do more?

Use other finger plays or verses that focus on other parts of the body.

Finger Flicks

Hands can be used to play all kinds of games. "Finger Flicks" lets the child predict which finger is the most accurate in scoring points. It's also a natural lead-in to inventing other games. How creative are your little people? You'll be impressed!

What to do

1. Cut and label openings as shown in the illustration. Place box on the floor against the wall.
2. Draw a shooting line with chalk or make a line with tape.
3. Ask a child to predict which finger will be the most accurate in scoring points.
4. The child then puts the object on the firing line and strikes the object with the finger predicted to be the most accurate.
5. The points are counted. Possible points with one shot are 1-4.
6. Each child gets one shot.
7. Were the predictions accurate?
8. Try again using another finger. Find which finger is the most accurate. Is it the same for everyone?
9. Predict how far your best finger can hit the object.

Want to do more?

What other objects can you flick with your fingers? Try rolling a small ball to score points. Is it easier or harder than flicking something flat? Which is the most accurate?

Language you can use

finger
hit
strike
predict
far
farther
farthest
distance
accuracy
points
score
stronger
strongest

Things you will need

box to place on table or on a smooth floor (see illustration)

scissors
tape or chalk

small, smooth wooden disks, such as checkers

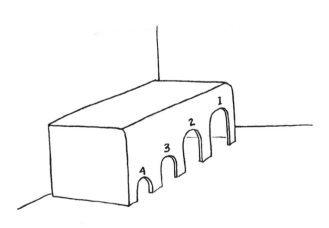

Quick Catch: Reaction Time

Language you can use

reaction
react
stimulus
response
fast
quick

Things you will need

rulers

a chart to record reaction time

Reaction time is the time it takes for your mind and body to react after a stimulus has been presented. When a ball is thrown at you it takes a given period of time to see the throw, to have your brain see that event and then tell the hands and arms to come up into position to catch the ball. This reaction time is important to certain jobs and certain athletic activities. Reaction time can be measured and be improved with practice, to a certain point. How quick are you to react?

What to do

1. Give some examples of a person having to react quickly to some event: a door slamming in your face—you put your hands up to stop the door; someone throwing something at you without you knowing—you try to catch the object; falling down—you try to break the fall with your hands; batting a hard-thrown ball.

2. The amount of time required for each of us to see or hear an event and react in a given way to that observation is our reaction time. We can play a catch game with our fingers that can give us an idea how and what our reaction time is.

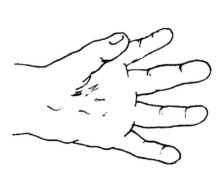

3. Show the children the way the ruler is held and how they should try to catch the ruler when you drop it. See the illustration for the proper positions. Place the thumb and finger so the ruler can slide easily. The bottom of the ruler should be even with the middle of the thumb and finger. Have one child watch your hand for the release of the ruler. When he sees the release, have him close his fingers to hold the ruler. The distance the ruler drops is a measurement of the time taken for reaction. The shorter the distance fallen, the better the reaction time.

4. Note each child's reaction time. If you have a child with a very slow reaction time, find a longer ruler. Reaction time is often related to athletic prowess.

Want to do more?

Make a chart of the reaction time of each child. Practice improves reaction time; start a practice session to see if practice does improve reaction time. Take a field trip to a table tennis area. Have some older students play table tennis. Observe reaction time.

A Hand Span

Each of us has a particular hand, foot, or body size that changes as we grow. Just like our height, the hand can be measured. Some of us have short, thick hands. Other hands are long and slender. Hands range in size and shape. So does the span. Piano players and good typists often have long fingers that stretch to form a larger span. Measuring your children's hand spans can show how varied such measurements can be.

What to do

1. Talk about hands. Some people have hands with long fingers, some people have short fingers, other people can stretch their hands very wide. Demonstrate this.
2. Let's find out about our hand spans by measuring them. Have the children lay their hands on paper, stretching them out. Trace each child's hand.
3. Measure each hand span using Unifix cubes or Cuisenaire rods. The latter is more accurate because of the smaller size increments.
4. Make a chart of the sizes by grouping common measurements. What size is most common?

Want to do more?

Is there a relationship between small hands and small bodies? Some people can be big but have small hands. Save the chart until later in the year to compare growth.

Language you can use

measure
stretch
span
variation

Things you will need

Unifix cubes or
Cuisenaire rods
butcher paper
marker

Snapping Fingers

Language you can use

snap
practice
friction
middle finger
thumb

Things you will need

a healthy hand
practice time
chart to record
who can snap
 marker

Some skills children learn as they grow have special meaning because they happened at a certain time or with a certain person. Some of those special skills are whistling, telling time, clapping hands, and the topic of this lesson, snapping fingers. Not an easy skill to learn because it takes practice and concentration, snapping fingers is not a normal school activity. But, why not? Snapping fingers is a learned task that can be taught and can be performed after practice. Most of us learn it during our lives, but can perform the task earlier if we are taught. Keeping this task a fun one is important, with the general idea that emphasizes practice as an absolute necessity. Another key is that some children require more practice to do a particular task than others and that is a part of life. Another task may be easy for them. Now snap to it!

What to do

1. Show the children how to snap. Snap your fingers several times. Talk about how people need to learn to snap their fingers because they want to call their dog, they want someone's attention (some think this is rude), or they want to keep time to music.
2. Ask if anyone can snap. Some may. Note these on your chart.
3. Now begin with individual instructions, working with sets of three or four children. Usually the dominant hand is the best snapping finger. Sometimes wetting the finger provides friction for the snap. They cannot just rub fingers together to form the friction to produce the snap. Snapping is a result of pressure and the sound made from the fingers slipping apart.
4. Note as each child is able to practice enough to be successful. For children having problems, enlist parental or other help. If a child has weak hand and finger muscles, snapping may be difficult or impossible. If a frustration level is reached, then a hand clap will have to suffice.

Want to do more?

Record in the chart all the times in hours or days that were required to be successful. Graph this result. Have the children teach their dog or pet to react to the snap. Snap to a song. "Old McDonald Had a Farm" is a great song to snap along.

> *Some folks have the knack for snapping,*
> *For some that skill is lacking.*
> *With some help from a friend,*
> *To show you how to begin,*
> *With some practice, you'll soon be*
> *snap-cracking.*

CHAPTER TWO

Huggers and Hoppers: How Arms and Legs Help You

Huggers and Hoppers: How Arms and Legs Help You

INFORMATION PLEASE

What bones are in the arm?

The arm is made up of a long bone (HUMERUS) that runs from the shoulder to the elbow, the two bones of the forearm (RADIUS and ULNA), the wrist bones, the hand bones and the finger bones.

What are the muscles?

There are 600 different muscles in the human body. The purpose of these muscles is to cause movement. The muscles move and make other parts of the body move. Every movement the body makes is done by muscles. Muscles work by tightening and contracting. When muscles contract, they become shorter and thicker and, in this way, exert a pull.

How do the arm muscles work?

The arm has two major muscles that work together. They cooperate. When one works, the other one rests. The muscle that bends the arm is called a FLEXOR. The muscle that extends the arm is called an EXTENSOR. The flexor (BICEPS) muscle on top of the upper arm makes the forearm move up, and the extensor (TRICEPS) muscle underneath the upper arm makes the forearm move down. When the biceps contracts and works, the triceps rests and relaxes.

What bones are in the leg?

The leg has a long bone (FEMUR). It runs from the hip to the knee. The lower leg has two bones (TIBIA and FIBULA) that run from the knee to the foot, where the ankle bones connect to the foot and toes bones. The knee has a special bone called the PATELLA. The bones of the leg are strong and sturdy because they must support the weight of the body and be involved in most of the actions that allow us to move, jump, and run.

How do the leg muscles work?

The leg has the largest muscles of the body and they do much work as we run and play. The RECTUS is the muscle on the front of the upper leg that allows us to lift our legs. On either side of the upper leg are the ADDUCTOR and ABDUCTOR muscles that let us move the legs apart and together. Much like the arm, the leg muscles must work in pairs to move the leg and rotate the body. Because these muscles do so much work, they use tremendous amounts of energy. Some of us have leg aches when we work or play too much. Resting causes the pain to disappear. Exercising too much can cause strain to be placed on the leg. The strain can cause the muscle to work incorrectly or to tighten. The muscles must then be rested.

Shivering

Shivering is a response of the muscles of the body to the cold. When you shiver, some of your muscles tighten and relax over and over again very quickly. The muscles, usually in the arms and legs, work without being told what to do. This is much like reflex action. When muscles work hard, it warms up our bodies. On a cold day, playing or running warm you up too, which means you will not shiver. Keeping active keeps shivering from happening.

Give Yourself a Hug

Hugs are used to express feelings of caring, love, and concern for others. We can use words to tell people how we feel. If it's all right with them, we can also use our arms. There is one person it's always all right to hug—yourself!

What to do

1. What is a hug? When do we hug? Whom do we hug? Why?
2. What parts of your body do you use to hug your friends and family?
3. How do you think others feel when you give them a hug? How do you feel when someone you like hugs you?
4. Do you ever feel good about something you have done? Why not give yourself a hug? Do you ever feel sad or lonely? That's another good time for a hug. Cross your arms in front of your body and hug away!

Want to do more?

Hug your dog, your cat, or other pets. What are some pets we can't hug? Hug by locking a finger with your friend's finger. A finger hug can be your special way of sharing feelings.

I can't hug a bug,
I can't hug a rug,
But I can always hug me.
When I'm feeling glad,
When I'm feeling sad,
I can always, always hug me.

Language you can use

love
care
concern
sad
happy
hug
feel
feelings
arms

Things you will need

people

Reach for the Stars

Language you can use

reach
stretch
high
higher

Things you will need

paper stars
tape

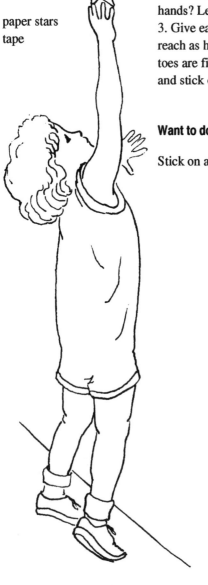

How high can you reach? Can you reach higher with one arm or both arms together? Let's reach for the stars and find out.

What to do

1. Discuss how arms are used for reaching. What are some times we use our ability to reach? Encourage the children to think of and demonstrate examples of reaching. Someone might reach to turn on a light. Another person might pretend to get a box of cereal out of a high cupboard.
2. What do the children think—can we reach farther with one hand or both hands? Let's reach for the stars and find out.
3. Give each child two paper stars with tape on the back. Have the children reach as high as they can with one hand and stick one star on the wall. Tiptoes are fine, but no jumping. Now reach as high as they can with both hands and stick on the other star. Which star is higher? Is it the same for everyone?

Want to do more?

Stick on a third star by jumping. Which star is the highest now?

The Little Star

Twinkle, twinkle, little star,
How I wonder what you are;
Up above the world, so bright,
Like a diamond in the night.

When the blazing sun is gone,
When it nothing shines upon,
Then you show your little light,
Twinkle, twinkle, all the night.

Then the traveller in the dark,
Thanks you for your tiny spark.

Tired, Tired, Tired

One will soon note after doing a bit of hard work that a direct relationship exists between muscles and the ability to do work for long periods. However, this fact does not usually hit the cranium until later in life, and maybe not even in adulthood. Another fact we will soon learn in our hard work is that muscles tire out. Our learning will tell us that lactic acid builds up in the muscles and this causes them to become inoperative. Can this happen to little muscles in a short period of time? Shall we see?

What to do

1. Discuss how the muscles are the parts of the body that do work. They can push, they can hold, they can lift. This activity is to see not how much you can lift, but how long you can lift.
2. Demonstrate how to hold the bucket of sand out in front of you with your arm extended. Start the timer and hold the bucket in the extended position until the arm is too tired to hold itself out. The mind may say to hold the bucket out, but the arm becomes too fatigued (tired) to obey the command.
3. Note on the chart the amount of time it took for each child's arm to tire.
4. Discuss how it feels for the arm to become tired. The muscles become fatigued and must be rested. Our bodies have a built-in mechanism to protect itself from overfatigue.

Want to do more?

Test to see if practice with lifting will increase the time one can lift. Visit a weight lifting session at the local gym. Have a weight lifter come in to share that hobby. Try holding the same weight in different arm positions. Is there a best way to use the arms to lift? Try the legs. Do they become tired of lifting as soon as arms? Can you determine the best way to use the legs to lift?

Muscles make up about half the weight of your whole body.

Language you can use

muscles
tire
fatigue
lift
hold

Things you will need

a sand bucket with a pint of sand in the bottom

a timer
a data table and marker

Circle Back Rubs

Language you can use

back rub
work
soft
hard
circle

Things you will need

people
paper and marker
optional—music

The arms have so many uses. Young children use them for throwing, holding, moving, climbing, hugging, and many other important things. Baseball players use their arms to pitch. Carpenters use their arms to hammer. Engineers use their arms to type at a computer. Most people have very useful jobs for their arms. This activity encourages children to use their arms and hands for an important job—giving their friends a back rub.

What to do

1. Ask a child to stand in front of you so you can show the group what a back rub is.
2. Help the children sit in a circle on the floor with everyone facing in the same direction. The circle should be close enough so that everyone is within easy reach of their neighbor's back.
3. Begin the back rub. You may wish to play relaxing music. The slower the music, the slower and softer the back rub is likely to be. After a short while, reverse the circle. This can become a relaxing part of the daily routine. It's a nice way for the children to nurture each other.
4. Arms can be used for helping and making people feel better. Can you think of other ways that you can use your arms? Make a list of ways children's arms are helpful.

Want to do more?

How can you use your legs? Can you give a back rub with legs? Make a list of ways that children's legs can be helpful.

> *I knead you,*
> *You knead me.*
> *We both can knead,*
> *So fine indeed.*

Wide World of Sports

We use our arms in a large variety of sports activities that are played by children and adults. This activity focuses on how our arms are used in the many skills that are developed as we play and participate in the wide world of sports.

What to do

1. Ask the children what sports activities they like. Answers will be varied, but some of the most common responses will be baseball, football, basketball, volleyball, swimming, tennis, bowling, dancing, and gymnastics.
2. Have the children demonstrate how they use their arms in the various sports activities that they name.
3. Let each child take a turn doing only arm movements of a sport of their choice. Other children attempt to identify the sport as they observe the arm movements of the demonstration.
4. Have children do a tally sheet of the activities to see which are the favorites of this particular group.

Want to do more?

Use the same procedure to identify how arms are used to work in the yard, in the house, at school.

Language you can use

arms
playing
games
sports
body part names
sports terms

Things you will need

children
tally sheets
marker

Bones Can't Hide

Language you can use

X-ray
broken
break
bones
doctor
fracture
cast
hospital
setting

Things you will need

X-rays of arm
and leg breaks
a removed cast
strips of paper
towel
flour and water
glue
dried twigs from
tree
X-ray machine
(see illustration)

The most frequently broken bones in children are the arm bones, then the collar bone. X-rays of these breaks can be obtained from doctors or clinics. The children may not be able to distinguish the break in some X-rays, in others they can; however, good X-rays do show the bones. You can use a hurt that many children may understand to talk about the long bones that are so important to movement and standing.

What to do

1. Discuss broken arms/legs with the children. Look at X-rays of broken bones. Ask children who have had a broken bone to share their experience, or bring in a child who has or had a broken bone. Bones break because of accidents. That is what happened to these unlucky people.
2. What happens when a bone breaks? You are taken to the hospital, a doctor looks at the arm, then they take an X-ray, and finally, a cast is put on the broken limb. Given time, the bone heals and the cast is removed.
3. Let's see if we can repeat the procedure for the children using a twig as a substitute for a broken arm.
4. The teacher hands the children twigs. Use strong twigs. The children break the twigs. It requires real force to break a twig (and a bone); the children can see that breaking a twig (bone) is difficult.
5. Place the twig in the X-ray device and lower it into the X-ray machine. Observe the break in the twig. The doctor recommends setting the twig (bone) and applying a cast.
6. Carefully take the twig to the cast table. Place the two ends close together (setting them). Put the cast on by wrapping paper towel strips coated with flour and water around the twig, creating a cast. Place this in the "recovery room" to dry.
7. Discuss the healing process with the children. Safety in the classroom will prevent most broken bones. Most accidents are a result of too much force in an unwanted direction. Running and falling are such incidents.

Want to do more?

Visit a hospital X-ray department. Look at many X-rays. Have someone with a cast come in to talk about broken bones. A visit by a doctor would be fun as the process evolves.

X-Ray. X-Ray
Looks inside.
X-Ray, X-Ray
Bones can't hide.

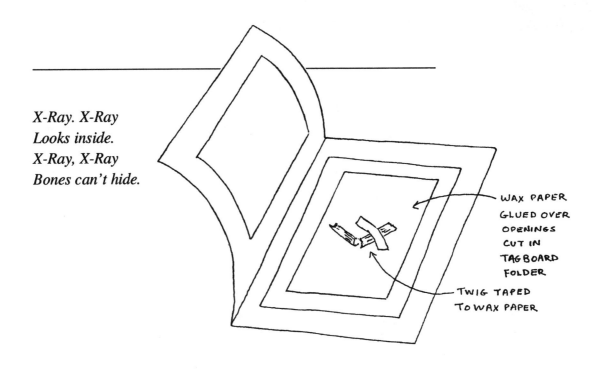

WAX PAPER
GLUED OVER
OPENINGS
CUT IN
TAGBOARD
FOLDER

TWIG TAPED
TO WAX PAPER

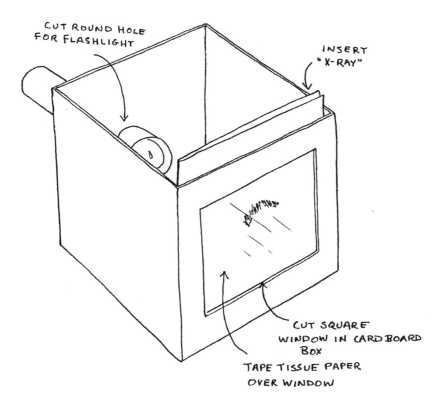

CUT ROUND HOLE
FOR FLASHLIGHT

INSERT
"X-RAY"

CUT SQUARE
WINDOW IN CARDBOARD
BOX

TAPE TISSUE PAPER
OVER WINDOW

What a Pair: Muscle Teamwork

Language you can use

palm
hand
arm
biceps
triceps
muscle
relax
contract
hard
soft

Things you will need

a chair and a table

Many young children enjoy showing off their arm muscles. They know how to bend their arm and make a fist to contract their biceps. The next time muscles are a topic of conversation, share this activity. It demonstrates the muscle movement called contraction. It also identifies how muscle pairs, specifically biceps and triceps, work together as a pair. One muscle relaxes while the other muscle works. What a team!

What to do

1. Can the children show you their arm muscles? Feel the hard part of your arm. That's called the biceps muscle.
2. Ask the children to sit in a chair next to a table.
3. Now place one hand, palm up, under the table and push upwards on the table.
4. Have them use their other hand to feel the front and back of their upper arm.
5. Which muscle is hard? The one in front or the one in back? The muscle that feels hard is called the biceps. When it is hard, it is contracted. The muscle in the back of the arm is called the triceps. It is soft and relaxed.
6. Now remove your hand from the bottom of the table and place your palm on the table top. Press down as hard as you can.
7. Now touch your upper arm muscles. Which one is hard now? Which one is contracted? Which one is relaxed?

Want to do more?

Do muscles in the legs work the same way?

> *Muscles never push,*
> *They only pull.*
> *We'd never josh you,*
> *And that's no bull.*

What Is an Arm's Length?

Arms are used for throwing, swinging, and holding, legs for running, kicking, and standing. The list of ways that arms and legs help us is virtually endless, but our arms and legs aren't. Just how long are they?

What to do

l. Stick the Unifix cubes together and demonstrate how to measure the arm.
2. Have the children work in pairs. Who do they think has the longer arm? Measure each other's arms and find out.
3. Measure legs in the same way.

Want to do more?

Make graphs from construction paper. Make the arms and legs of different colored paper. Have them measure things in arm lengths/leg lengths.

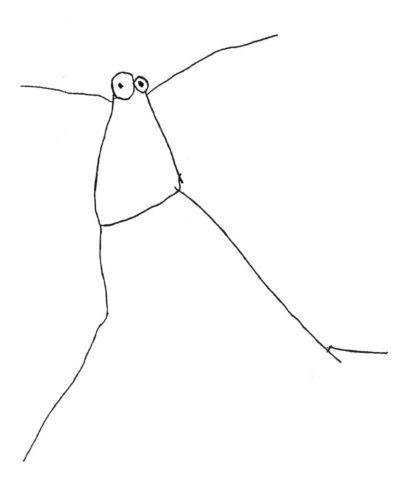

It's a Tossup

Language you can use

throw
carpet square
hard
soft
in
out
beside

Things you will need

carpet squares
beanbags

We use our arms when we throw. Children can practice this movement over and over as they refine the skill. This activity can be modified to accommodate both the very young child who is at the initial stage of throwing to the mature child. We will focus here on 2-5 year old children.

What to do

1. Give each child a beanbag and a carpet square to mark their personal space.
2. First an adult is the leader, giving directions such as:
- Stand on your carpet square.
- Stand behind your carpet square.
- Drop your beanbag on your carpet square.
- Throw your beanbag softly on your carpet square.
- Throw your beanbag hard on your carpet square.
- Toss your beanbag on the red square.
- Toss your beanbag on Charlie's square.
3. Let the children take turns being the leader.

Want to do more?

Repeat the activity emphasizing different concepts each time. Some ideas are over/under, top/bottom, beside/next to.

Let's Go Visit the Zoo Today: Moving With the Animals

Zoo animals move by running, jumping, crawling, and walking, just as humans do. This activity lets the children mimic animal movement and reinforces the concept that legs and feet are used similarly by creatures great and small.

What to do

1. Show the children pictures of a variety of animals with legs, such as a kangaroo, rabbit, cat, fox, horse, frog, monkey, and bear.
2. Which animal would they like to be first? Look at the picture closely. What do they know about how this animal moves? Let's all try it out.
3. Which animals move most like we do? Which animals move very differently? How do animals with no legs move?

Want to do more?

Take a field trip to the zoo. Photograph the animals the children actually see. Repeat the movement activity based upon the children recalling their observations. Play and repeat the activity at a later date. Ask the children to observe and attempt to identify the animal movement being acted out by other children. Sing the following song to the tune of "Here We Go Round the Mulberry Bush."

Let's go visit the zoo today
Zoo today, zoo today
Let's go visit the zoo today
What animals will we see?

This is the way the kangaroos jump...
Chasing one another...

This is the way the tiger prowls...
Sneaking through the grasses...

This is the way the monkey climbs...
Looking for adventure...

The big old snake slithers along...
Looking for some dinner...

Language you can use

move
zoo
animals
pretend

Things you will need

animal photographs

Weather Walk

Language you can use

season
fall
autumn
winter
spring
summer
cold
warm
hot
windy
rainy
sunny
snow
shivering
sweaty

Things you will need

children

Take a fantasy journey to recall the sights, sounds, and feelings of seasons past. What was the weather like at Halloween? What kind of clothes do you wear in the summer? What happens to the grass in spring? Do the children know what season will be next?

What to do

1. Discuss the seasons: summer, fall, winter, spring. Stand in a large circle.
2. How do we walk at various times of the year?
3. Let's pretend as we go through the seasons. We can walk as we remember fall, winter, spring, and summer days.
4. For example:

Fall—Walking though leaves, catching them as they fall from the trees.

Winter—Walking in the snow, feeling cold, slippery-walk on ice.

Spring—Walking in the woods, watching the sun as it peeks through branches that are filled with buds. Suddenly it starts to rain.

Summer—It's a very hot day. We are walking on the beach. The sand is very hot. Let's hurry to the water. Oh, it's much cooler now. Let's splash through the water.

Want to do more?

Draw pictures or make collages about the different seasons.

I like autumn—crunchy leaves,
Colors falling out of trees,
I like autumn.

I like winter—snow is nice,
Slipping, sliding on the ice,
I like winter.

I like spring—pink and green,
Wind and rain on everything,
I like spring.

I like summer—skies of blue,
So many lovely things to do,
I like summer.

Walk Along Tales

We walk in various ways, depending on our moods and on the environment. This fantasy activity reviews various ways we walk and what those ways express. It also encourages children to create new variations of walking. The children can be remarkably dramatic as they play out their moods.

What to do

1. We walk in many ways. Let's try to think of the ways we walk at different times and in different places. Have the children describe various ways that they walk as they move from place to place. How do they walk outside on a warm, sunny day? How do they walk when they're soooo tired?

2. Describe a situation and ask the children to show how they might walk. For example:

- The baby is sleeping; we don't want to awaken the baby. Let's tiptoe quietly as we pass the baby's room.
- We are in a parade. We are marching down the street. There's your mom! Wave hello!
- We are giants. We take big giant steps as we walk through the forest.
- We are trying to awaken our baby doll who has been sleeping all day. Let's walk and stomp our feet. Perhaps that will awaken her.
- We're in a hurry to get some ice cream. Let's walk fast!

3. Ask the children to show some other ways to walk from place to place.

Want to do more?

Pantomime other situations, using the whole body. Act out activities for others to guess. Can people guess the way you are pretending to feel?

Language you can use

create
pretend
different
sad
happy
tired
other descriptive words

Things you will need

children

Penguin Running

Language you can use

arms
demonstrate
balance

Things you will need

an open area with few obstacles or things to bump into

At first glance, the act of running would appear to be rather easy and simple to explain and to do. Actually, running is a rather complicated act that our human body makes look simple, especially for the active young person. So let us try to make running a bit more difficult by changing how some of the body parts—the arms in particular—can change the way one runs and the ease with which one runs....

What to do

1. Have the children run across the area you have selected.
2. When they return, start a discussion about running. They will be delighted to run, and you can tell them that running and learning about running is what you are about to do.
3. Ask for a volunteer to run. Select one and ask that child to run to a specific object and return.

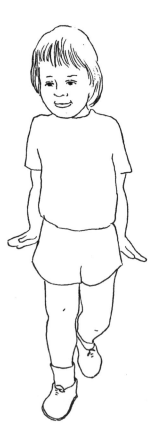

4. During the run ask the children to point out the characteristics of running. You will have to help the children develop descriptors. Some descriptions will include the length of the stride, the way the body moves, how one leg moves in relation to the other, and finally, how the arms react to each stride. The arms are very important to running, which is one focus of this running lesson. Ask others to run until the complete running pattern of most children is determined.
5. The arms, in the forward and backward motion in running, help to stabilize the body in an upright position. If you carry things or hold your arms down to the side, running is more difficult and you feel much more clumsy. So having defined running, ask the children to run across to the other side of the playground in a normal manner, and return with hands held down to the side (model this for the children).
6. When they return, have them indicate which running style is easier to do and feels more comfortable. Which style of running feels funny?

Want to do more?

Hold your hands over your head. Run with your arms moving in exact rhythm with your body. Have a track runner come over and demonstrate running. Watch a video of track races. Is it easier to hold your arms still in fast or slow running? Discuss safety in running, especially running with something in your arms. Is it safer to run with your arms full or empty?

> *Frogs hop. Ducks waddle.*
> *Penguins run all wiggle waggle.*
> *Penguins slide and penguins swim*
> *And wiggle back on shore again.*

Balls of Fun: Exploring Attributes of Spherical Objects in Flight

Kicking balls is fun. Sports activities such as soccer depend on kicking expertise. While the physical activity is important to this lesson, predicting expected outcomes is the primary focus. How do the various attributes of the collection of balls affect kicking distance? What about color? Outside in the sun, color is not important. In a dark room it may matter quite a bit.

What to do

1. Ask the children to describe and compare all the balls in a variety of ways. Try comparing size, weight, material, color, softness, or texture.
2. Which attributes do the children think might affect the distance the balls can be kicked? What do they expect to happen and why?
3. Kick the balls. What happened? How accurate were the predictions?

Want to do more?

What are the predictions about throwing the balls? Try predicting the outcome with a new set of balls. Does experience improve accuracy?

Language you can use

descriptive words relating to size, weight, texture, color, etc. measure compare

Things you will need

five different balls such as a basketball, beach ball, ping-pong ball, sponge ball, playground ball, or whatever is available

1, 2, 3 Jump

Language you can use

sideways
forward
backward
hop
jump
measure
far
farther
farthest

Things you will need

space to jump
objects to measure the length of each jump, such as string, blocks, or Unifix cubes

paper and marker to record your information

How many ways are there to jump? The children will create quite a few. Among those that may be suggested are the one-legged jump, the two-legged jump, the forward jump, the triple jump, the backward one- or two-legged jump, the jump and turn, and the sideways jump. How many others can your children invent? So what about all these types of jumping? Which will carry you the farthest in a single bound?

What to do

1. Talk about jumping. How many ways can we think of to jump? As a child comes up with an idea, encourage the other children to try it.
2. After exploring all these jumping ideas, it's time to do some measuring.
3. Have each child choose a way to jump. Use your measuring device to record the length of the jump. Try another type of jump and measure its distance. Which jump works best—covers the greatest distance—for each child?
4. Is there a jump that works best for most children?

Want to do more?

Practice allows us to improve our athletic performances. Have the children practice their jumping and try to beat their own jump records. Does practice improve children's jumping? Make a graph for each person, for each jump. Is there a relationship between leg length and jump distance? The way to jump the farthest may not be the most fun. What do the children choose as their favorite jumps? Which way can they jump the most jumps in a row?

Jump high, jump low
How far can you go?
Run and jump, skip and jump
Can you land without a bump?
Hop on one foot. Jump on two.
Show me a jump that's right for you.

Walking Then and Now

We use our legs to move from one place to another. From the onset of walking as infants, we use this locomotor skill on a daily basis throughout our lifetime. This activity gives children an opportunity to observe how this movement skill (walking) is developed and refined as time passes, and as we grow older. Mature walking is usually achieved between the fourth and seventh year.

What to do

1. Remember when you were a little baby? How did you move around? (Parents carried you, crawled.) Do you remember when you began to walk? Was it hard to do?
2. Let's look at some pictures from home. Pictures of you as babies when you began to walk. If they are available, watch some home videos of the children as babies.
4. Do you remember walking like that? Do you walk like that now? What has changed as you have grown older? (We can walk better, faster, further now.)
5. How have your legs and feet changed? (Bigger, longer, stronger)
6. Form a circle. Pretend that you are a baby again. Walk like a baby.
7. Now walk like you did when you came to school today. We certainly do walk better now than we did then, don't we?
8. Do you think your walking skills will keep getting better or worse? Why? What changes do you think will make walking better or worse? Discuss how some very old people walk.

Want to do more?

Compare how baby animals walk to how human babies walk.

Dance, little baby, dance up high,
Never mind, baby, mother is by;
Crow and caper, caper and crow,
There, little baby, there you go.

Up to the ceiling, down to the ground,
Backwards and forwards, round and round;
Dance, little baby, and mother will sing,
With the merry chorus, ding, ding, ding!

Language you can use

baby
crawl
stand
walk
slow
foot
shaky
fell
rock
strong
big
bigger
longer
muscles
bones
legs
feet
change
time
older
younger
life cycle

Things you will need

photos or videos of walking and crawling

It's Mommy carrying Jenna

Space Walk

Language you can use

legs
feet
fast
slow
cautious
gooey
stuck
squish

names of planets
and space shuttle
astronauts

Things you will need

children
chairs

"Let's pretend..." is the start of many play experiences for children. This bit of pretending encourages the children to explore the variety of ways in which their bodies can move. They fly in a spaceship to a strange and unfamiliar planet. What's even more amazing is what covers the surface of this planet. Our legs move in a variety of ways depending on the surface we're walking on.

What to do

1. Children and teachers prepare spaceships for take-off. Set the stage by having the children lay their chairs on the floor and sit in their chairs. This is how the astronauts are seated for take-off. Count down and liftoff.
2. Fly by planets in the solar system. Talk about their colors and shapes as you "pass them by."
3. See a strange planet that is not part of the solar system. Decide to land and explore.
4. Put on space suits, open the doors of spaceship and climb down to the surface of the planet. (See "Space Helmets" in *Mudpies to Magnets*.)
5. Do an exploration walk. This planet has many unusual surfaces. The children and teacher walk on these surfaces as they explore the planet. The teacher describes the surface, and the children modify their walking movements accordingly, for example, hot sand, sticky bubble gum, cold snow, slippery mud, wet glue, sharp nails, eggshells, thick, chocolate milk shake.
6. It's time to go back home. What should we name this planet?

Want to do more?

Use other adventures to help children use their bodies in a variety of ways. Where would they like to go?

Quirky Jerks

When someone taps you just below the knee, your leg will jerk upward. You can't stop this from happening no matter what you do. It is the result of nerve impulses traveling from the spinal cord directly to the muscle. These impulses are not controlled by the brain. When the tendon just below the kneecap is given a sharp tap, your knee will jerk. This is called a reflex reaction.

What to do

1. Tell the children that you can show them how to kick a ball without even trying. They will not have to kick it on their own. You can make a leg move even if a child is thinking very hard about not letting it move.
2. Ask a child to sit on the table or chair. Ask the children to predict how far the ball will go if the person tries **not** to kick it. It is likely that most of the children will think that the ball will not move.
3. Place the ball in front of the child's foot. Tell the child not to kick the ball. Think hard, "I will not kick the ball!"
4. Strike the tendon just below the knee cap. What happens? How far did the ball go? Were your predictions correct?

Want to do more?

Set up a target. Check how accurate a reflexive kick is compared to a voluntary kick.

Language you can use

reflex
knee
jerk
kick
strike
upward
brain
control
stop
nerve
impulse
kneecap

Things you will need

small rubber mallet

soccer ball

a table or chair so a child can sit with both legs suspended approximately 5 centimeters (2") from the floor

Pick a Quick Kick: Prediction

Language you can use

hard
soft
harder
softer
force

Things you will need

a number of kick balls

a flat grassy spot blocks to serve as markers

Force is an important idea to the physicist and engineer. Having an early working knowledge of this concept would be helpful for the budding scientist. When force is described by the scientists, they usually refer to that which changes, produces, or stops the motion of a body.

What to do

1. Explain to the children that force is a word that scientists use to explain motion.
2. When we kick an object, we are using force provided by our legs to propel or drive a kick ball. The ball will go further if more force is applied; that is, the harder you kick, the more force you have.
3. Have the children line up and show you how they would kick the ball if it were a soft kick. What would happen to the ball? They should say that it will not go far. Now have them kick the ball softly. Place a marker on the spot the ball reached.

4. Now have the children pretend to kick the ball harder. Not as hard as they can, but harder than the first kick. Have them predict how far the ball will go. They should point to a place further than the last kick. Each time, kick the ball harder.
5. Now have them follow the same procedure with the hardest kick (the most force). They should predict a point out beyond the last kick.

Want to do more?

Use the same procedure to discuss force by throwing.

Here's Looking at You: How Eyes See

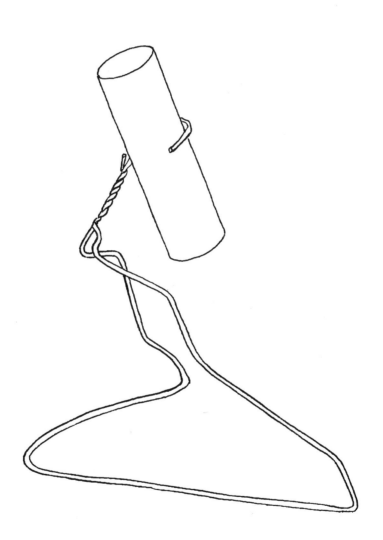

Here's Looking at You: How Eyes See

INFORMATION PLEASE

The human being has developed ways of evaluating and observing a constantly changing external environment. This development of sensory devices has evolved as humans have taken their place on the planet. The chief sensory device for people is the visual mechanism of the eyes. Once used to see fast moving or dangerous conditions for early primates, the eyes now serve in reading, computing, and pleasure. The eyes have become a tool of modern humans and with that importance has come increased concern over their care and maintenance. So we must teach children the beginning of an understanding of how the eye functions and some rudiments of eye care.

How do the eyes work?

The eyes must receive light from a light source as it reflects off objects in the environment. Light, and the colors represented by light, strikes objects and moves into the eye. The light passes through the CORNEA, a thin transparent cover over the eye, into a watery substance called the AQUEOUS HUMOR. On either side of the aqueous humor is a muscular circular disc called the IRIS. The iris is the colored area in the eye. In the iris are color pigments that give us our eye color. The iris is really a muscle that expands and contracts to allow additional light into the eye. The dark central portion is called the PUPIL and is where the light passes through the LENS into the central watery yet semisolid portion (VITREOUS HUMOR) on its way to strike the RETINA. The retina turns the light signal into nerve impulses that can be sent to the brain via the OPTIC NERVE.

When the position of the lens in relation to the retina is balanced, a person has normal vision. If the eye is too short and the image passing through the lens is projected to a place behind the eye, the condition is termed FARSIGHTEDNESS. If the image passing through the lens is focused in front of the retina, the condition is labeled NEARSIGHTEDNESS. These problems are caused by the eye not being able to accommodate (change shape) for all the environmental situations presented. Glasses or contacts are used to correct these conditions. Other abnormalities can be found in the eyes of children, but these two are the most common.

Other eye facts include BLINKING, which is a reflex action. We each have our own blinking rate. TEARS come from a small duct in the corners of the eye. Tear fluid is important in keeping the eyes wet. You cry tears when a nerve in the eye is stimulated. Emotions, coughing, and sneezing cause us to cry. We think that humans are the only animals that cry for emotional reasons. Humans do not see colors in the dark. The most commonly visited eye professionals are OPTOMETRISTS and OPHTHAL-

MOLOGISTS. A visit to either one of these can provide a field trip, a class visit and demonstration, or good literature on vision care.

Nearly half of all blindness can be prevented. An important task of teachers of young children is to determine the visual state of their children. Simple tests and activities can be used to determine whether sight deficiencies will inhibit children's learning. Early detection of visual problems can help in assessing and addressing children's learning patterns. But teachers cannot be expected to evaluate a child's eye problems; that is the job of a professional.

It is estimated that one in every 20 preschool children in the U.S. has a vision problem which, if left uncorrected, can lead to needless loss of sight. For some of these children, such as those with amblyopia ("lazy eye"), discovery and treatment before school age is extremely important. Just because a child doesn't complain about his eyesight, you can't assume that there aren't any vision problems. Most children believe that the way they see is the way everyone sees—even if vision is blurred, doubled, or through only one eye.

Some signs of possible eye trouble in children — from the National Society to Prevent Blindness

Any concern about abnormalities in the appearance of the eyes should be investigated further. Some examples include the following:

Behavior:
- Rubs eye excessively.
- Shuts or covers one eye; tilts head or thrusts head forward.
- Has difficulty with reading or other close-up work.
- Blinks more than usual or is irritable when doing close-up work.
- Is unable to see distant things clearly.
- Squints eyelids together or frowns.

Appearance:
- Crossed eyes.
- Red-rimmed, encrusted, or swollen eyelids.
- Inflamed or watery eyes.
- Recurring sties, infections on eyelids.

Complaints:
- Eyes itch, burn, or feel scratchy.
- Cannot see well.
- Dizziness, headaches, or nausea following close-up work.
- Blurred or double vision.

If a child exhibits one or more of these signs of possible eye trouble, professional eye care should be sought. A professional eye examination for every child, including those who do not display any signs of eye trouble, is recommended shortly after birth, by six months of age, before entering school (age four or five), and periodically throughout the school years.

Backwards Button Up

Mirrors can provide any number of exciting visual activities. Mirrors reverse images. The children watch themselves in the mirror as they experiment with this phenomenon. They'll be amazed at how tricky the simplest things can be.

What to do

l. Have the children perform some of these activities by looking ONLY in the mirror.

> Fasten and unfasten a button.
> Put lids on the jars.
> Put caps on the markers.
> Trace a circle.
> See their feet.

2. Talk about what happens. What makes the tasks so hard? What have you discovered about mirror images?

Want to do more?

Try to put a puzzle together. As the children become more skilled, choose more complex tasks. What happens when they try to draw looking only in the mirror? Older children may be able to draw a mirror image of themselves.

Mirrors reverse the things I see.
They make the world look backwards to
  me.
Easy things become confusing.
I can't tell which hand I'm using.

Language you can use

mirror
image
reverse
reflection
backwards

Things you will need

large mirror
hung on the wall
30 cm (one foot)
off the floor

a chair placed
in front of the
mirror

objects in a box
beside the chair

clipboard with
picture of a circle

crayons
jars with lids
markers with
caps

Complementary Colors

4

Language you can use

complementary
color names
image
visual

When you look at colors, what do you really see? Knowing a little about how the eyes, in conjunction with the brain, are able to work can offer all of us a peek into the complexity of our human body. One of the strange attributes of sight is that our eyes not only see a color, but in some instances our brain receives an afterimage of a color. It is the complement of the color observed. The complementary color of red is green, yellow is purple, and blue is orange.

Things you will need

sheets of white paper for each child

sets of colored construction paper cut in three cm (one inch) squares in colors of yellow, green, blue, purple, orange, plus other vivid colors

What to do

1. Pass out the set of colored squares and white paper to each of the children. Tell them that you would like to show them a very special trick that the eyes can do.
2. Take the white sheet and lay it down flat on the table. Take a colored square and lay it in the center of the sheet. Holding your eyes from 30 to 60 cm (one to two feet) away, look very hard at the square for several seconds. Then very gently close your eyes and allow the afterimage to appear. What will appear is the complement of the color. If you look at red, green will be the afterimage.
3. Encourage the children to experiment with different colors and talk about what they see.
NOTE: The image takes a few seconds to appear and children need to be able to identify colors. Some people cannot do this activity because they cannot receive the image. Color blindness will also change things, as you might expect.

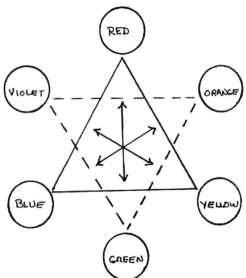

Want to do more?

Try the new and strange colors found in clothes, gift wrapping, cards and such. Put cards together and see what happens. You can make a complementary color American flag. What are the colors? Yes! Green, black, and orange. Try it!

The normal human eye can distinguish about seven million variations of color.

Make It Big—Make It Small, Eyeglasses Do It All

All kinds of people wear glasses—young children, older children, teenagers, and adults. What do glasses do? How do they help us? Are they all alike or are they different? Glasses are made of lenses (plastic or glass) that help to make things look bigger, smaller, or in other ways more focused. This activity introduces children to glasses by allowing them to use a few pairs of glasses to see how they function. Some people cannot focus their eyes on things that are a long way off. This is because the lens in one or both of their eyes focuses the image in front of the retina so the image that forms on the retina is blurred. This is called nearsightedness (myopia). It can be corrected by wearing glasses with concave lenses. Other people cannot focus on things close to them because the lens forms a clear image behind the retina. This is called farsightedness (hypermetropia), and can be corrected with convex lenses. If you can find glasses used to correct astigmatism, the children can see another type used by many people. An eye doctor or optometrist will probably help you collect a set of glasses for your classroom experience.

What to do

1. Talk about glasses. If you wear them, talk about your experience. Some of us have eyes that do not function as well as they should. This is not a problem unless we have to perform tasks that require precise vision, for example reading. Encourage the children who wear glasses to talk about their experiences. Who has family members or friends who wear glasses?
2. This activity will allow the children to try on a number of pairs of glasses to see how individual sight is affected by the glasses. If the child has normal vision, the glasses will cause different sight experiences.
3. Talk about the care of glasses. They are special tools that need to be taken care of by all of us. Plastic lenses can be scratched. Glass lenses can break. Frames can be bent or broken.
4. Look at the thickness of the lenses. For myopia, the thicker the glass, the more nearsighted the wearer.
5. Lay the glasses on a sheet of words at the table. Bring the glasses slowly away from the sheet. What happens? The words should vary in size as the glasses are moved away and towards the words. That is how they help the eye. It is more complicated than that, but this explanation will have to do until they are older.
6. Put the glasses on and look around the room. What do the glasses do to your vision? Can you see better or worse? Go through all the pairs. Find the glasses used for astigmatism. Move the lenses around to see the variations ground into the same lens.

Language you can use

glasses
sight
farsighted-ness/hyper-metropia
nearsighted-ness/myopia
correct
vision
focus
blurry
clear

Things you will need

several pairs of old glasses for a variety of needs

a page of letters or a page from a book

Want to do more?

Discuss eye doctors or visit one. Use an eye chart. Have someone come in to do a preliminary eye screening with the entire class. Bring in examples of contact lenses; demonstrate how these are similar to glasses. Show the hard and soft lenses. Have someone come in and demonstrate how the contacts are put in the eye.

People have been wearing eyeglasses for more than 700 years.

The Eyes Have It

Language you can use

words descriptive of the children in your class

identify
name
characteristics
attributes
describe

Things you will need

children
paper and marker

"The Eyes Have It" will help children to observe and to develop questioning skills. This activity provides an opportunity to talk about similarities and differences in a warm and positive way. Eventually, the children will move from random guessing to more astute questions.

What to do

1. Have the children form a circle in the room so they can see each other well.
2. Tell the group that they are going to use their eyes to try to find the mystery person in the class. They must do this by asking the teacher questions about each other to try to guess who the teacher has chosen as the mystery person.
3. The questions must be asked one at a time and must be able to be answered by a yes or a no. Each question must be about a physical observation that the children can make about each other, characteristics that they can see. For example, does this person have blond hair? Does this person have on tie shoes? Does this person wear glasses?
4. Once the person has been identified (at first this may take a while), make a list of the attributes we can see that distinguish the mystery child from the other children.
5. Select another child and repeat the game. Choose a few mystery children each day. Skills will improve as the children enjoy the guessing and observing game.

Want to do more?

Try the activity with objects in the classroom, outdoors, in automobiles, with attributes of dinosaurs, letters, nature pictures, or numbers, and so on.

You Aren't What You See—Concave and Convex Mirrors

Language you can use

concave
convex
flat
reflection
mirror
look
see
smaller
larger

Things you will need

a convex mirror
(truck bubble
mirror)

a concave mirror
(shaving or
make-up mirror)

a flat mirror
everyday objects
a spoon

When rays of light hit a surface or an object, they bounce back off. This is called reflection. Flat, shiny surfaces produce the best reflections. Most mirrors are made of flat sheets of highly polished glass with a shiny silver coating behind them. Some mirrors are not flat. They are curved. This activity explores how flat and curved mirror reflections are received by the eye.

What to do

1. Place the three types of mirrors in the science center. Display them side by side. This can be done by hanging them at eye level or mounting them on a board hung at eye level. Show the children the three mirrors.
2. Provide a number of interesting objects for the children to examine in the mirrors.
3. After several days of experimentation, ask the children to talk about what they have discovered about the mirrors. How are the mirrors alike? How are they different? How are the images different? How are the images alike? You may want to point out that the convex mirror (truck bubble mirror) is curved outward like the back of a spoon (show the spoon). Compare the convex mirror to the flat mirror. The image will be smaller on the convex mirror that gathers light from a wide area. It gives drivers a good view of what is happening behind them. However, the images appear further away than they actually are.
4. As you compare the concave mirror to the flat mirror, explain that the concave mirror curves inward like the inside of a spoon (show the spoon). It reflects an image that is larger than the one seen in the flat mirror. Concave mirrors are used most frequently for make-up and shaving mirrors. They are also used for telescopes.

Want to do more?

Which type of mirror or mirrors do you have and use at home? The mirror reflects our image. Does it also reflect our feelings? How?

> *I went up one pair of stairs,*
> *Just like me.*
> *I went up two pairs of stairs,*
> *Just like me.*
> *I went into a room,*
> *Just like me.*
> *I looked in the mirror,*
> *Just like me.*
> *And there I saw a monkey,*
> *Just like me.*

How Far Can You See?

Language you can use

far
near
shape and color
names
distance

Things you will need

three blocks of different colors

cards with shapes drawn in black

a large outdoor open area

Sight is a wonderful sense and allows us to enjoy so much of our environment. We see color, shape, size, and movement with our eyes to help us interpret what is happening in the world. Is there a distance at which the eyes are unable to do their jobs? Do those distances vary with the sight job being done? Can you see color over a greater distance than you can see symbols? Let's see if there is a difference.

What to do

1. Before doing this activity with the children, you must try this out for yourself. Set up the series of objects in plain sight on a board about waist high. Place three blocks of different colors side by side. Place three shape cards side by side. Discover the distances at which you can discern the various objects.
2. Take the children for a walk, and as you do, talk about seeing objects of different sizes, shapes, and colors. Look at things up close and far away.
3. Far-away objects are harder to see. Which is harder to see—shape, color, size, or symbols?
4. Approach the objects that were set up earlier. Tell them about the sets of objects on the board. Talk about what you see as you walk closer.
5. Mark the spot where the first attribute is distinguished, then the next, and so on. As a child picks up an attribute, see if the rest of the class agrees. You may have to walk closer to have all the children see the attribute.
6. Discuss the need for having certain sight abilities for certain jobs. Talk about how glasses or binoculars may be used to enhance vision.

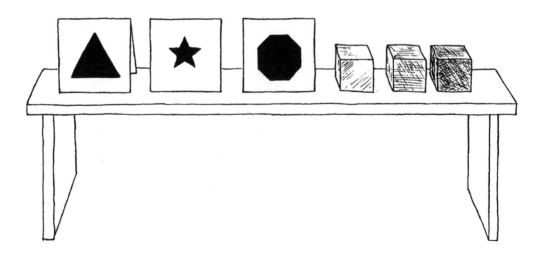

Want to do more?

Try to think of other attributes that can be determined farther or nearer than the ones you have experienced. Shades, reflection, movement are such attributes. Try to camouflage some of the items. Experiment with binoculars. Try other objects.

Touch and Tell

This activity lets children use the sense of touch as they attempt to identify their friends in the classroom. It also lets children experience the importance of sight and how they rely upon it. Children who are blind develop a keen sense of touch and are required to use it continuously.

What to do

1. Blindfold a child.
2. The teacher chooses another child to stand next to the blindfolded child.
3. The blindfolded child feels the other child's face, hair, clothing, shoulders, arms, and legs.
4. The blindfolded child is then asked to identify the child he or she is touching.

Want to do more?

Try to identify objects in the room, using the same procedure.

> *Eyes aren't the only way to see.*
> *My hands can find my friends for me.*
> *When I feel ears and face and hair,*
> *My hands can tell me who is there.*

Language you can use

identify
touch
tell
describe

Things you will need

blindfold

A Dim View—
Colors in the Dark

Language you can use

color names
light
dark
dim

Things you will need

box with a hand-sized hole in the side near the bottom (see illustration)

six different colored blocks of the same size

flashlight

The eyes are wonderful organs. We use them to tell us how many, what color, what shape, what size—all the characteristics needed to differentiate between toys, friends, parents, everything. Some characteristics are not nearly so easy to perceive when there is little or no light. If you want to wear your blue shirt tonight and the light is off as you choose it, you might pick out the wrong shirt if the shirts are all the same design. You don't believe that you cannot see colors at night? Well, try this experiment.

What to do

1. Show the children the blocks. Talk about how the eyes tell us the color of each block. What are the colors they see? Notice how clear and pretty the colors are in the bright light. As the light becomes dimmer and dimmer, our ability to discern color diminishes. Dim the lights and compare the color.
2. How well do eyes work when the light is very dim? Select six blocks and have one of the children come up and identify the colors. After the child has identified the colors, place the blocks in the back of the box. Now tell the child to look into the box, reach in, and bring out the (blue) block.
4. Unless the child does the picking by pure chance, there is little likelihood that the blue block will be selected. The lack of light will prevent the selection of the correct color no matter how hard the child tries to see in the box.
5. Reinforce the fact that human eyes don't work well in the dark. Identifying colors is especially hard.

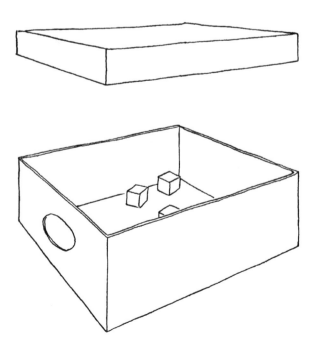

Want to do more?

Have the children experiment on a night walk with their parents. What colors do they see? Have them draw a picture of something at night.

Humans cannot see colors in the dark.

Eye Color Your Eyes

Genetics is an area in biology. A geneticist studies traits that are passed from the parent to the offspring. The geneticist who makes these studies looks for inherited traits that can be useful for a variety of reasons. Modern medicine is discovering that such traits are helpful in identifying and treating a variety of diseased and abnormalities. Knowing about the effects of the genes on the human body will become common knowledge as the study of humans continues. Eye color was one of the first traits to be explored in genetics. The young child's first look into the field of genetics can also be the study of eyes. Brown eyes are the most common, hazel or green the next, and blue the least common. What does your class have?

What to do

1. Each of us has features and characteristics that distinguish us from each other. Have the children identify some of these traits.
2. When the children have discovered that eye color is an important trait for each of them, determine what colors are found in eyes.
3. Eye color is determined by the pigment found in the eye's iris. You may want to draw an eye on the board and describe the parts they will see when looking at their friends' eyes to identify the color.
4. Pair off the children and give each child a face picture. The children will look at their friend's eyes and color the picture appropriately. The teacher can walk around, putting names on the pictures. When the eye color has been identified, have the children look at their partner and color the rest of the head with appropriate colors.
5. When they have finished coloring their friend's face, exchange the pictures. As the exchange is made have each say, "Here is your face picture_____(child's name); you have _____ (eye color) colored eyes."
6. Group the pictures by eye color. Determine which group has the greatest number and the least. Are any the same? Use the pictures to make a graph.

Want to do more?

Give the children one picture to complete for each family member. Look at eye color dominance in families. Please be sure to be sensitive to the diversity of family structures within your class. Large eyes and long lashes are also dominant. Eye safety can be introduced at this time.

Language you can use

genetics
blue
hazel
green
brown
inherit
trait
iris

Things you will need

large faces drawn on a sheet of paper and duplicated

different colored crayons, including those for each of the eye colors

Scope It Out: Eye Helpers

In scientific work, the unaided eye does not always provide enough vision to do some of the jobs that are required. Scientists have developed machines that will help the eyes. Some of those tools are binoculars, telescopes, hand lenses, microscopes, and cameras. Each of these devices uses lenses to enlarge objects for us to see. The glasses used by many of us are examples of a device created to aid the eye in its work. Introducing some of the eye helpers to your children is a way to begin early discovery in science.

What to do

1. Locate and bring in as many of the eye helpers as you can find. If you cannot find the real thing, find a picture. Set up stations so that the children can experience the eye helper instruments. Put an experienced adult at each station to help the children adjust the instrument to obtain maximum efficiency. Help the children be successful in looking through the eye tools. If they cannot close an eye when needed, help them cover an eye.
2. Play and pretend machines can be made for some of the tools that the children have been using. These can be made from paper rolls. Prepare a binocular table by giving each child two toilet paper rolls glued together. They can decorate their eye helpers.
3. A telescope can be made from single rolls. Making a telescope to look at things close up will require a shorter paper roll. If something very far away is to be observed, choose a very long roll.
4. Use a coat hanger to create a stand for a toilet paper tube that will serve as a microscope (see illustration). A variety of hand lenses can be collected for experimentation.

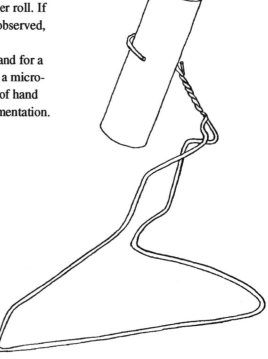

Want to do more?

Take a field trip out to the schoolyard and have the children try out their eye helpers. Talk about whether they are looking far away or up close. Visit places where the instruments are used regularly.

How Big Is Your Pupil?

The size of the eye's pupil changes with the amount of light hitting the surface of the eye. The iris is the muscled area that forms the colored portion of the eye. It contracts or expands with the light intensity. The pupil is the clear space behind the lens and the dark part you see in the center of the eye. The darker it is, the wider the pupil becomes in an effort to admit more light.

What to do

1. Explain that the eyes have a special mechanism that helps us to see. When it gets dark, the pupil of the eye becomes larger to allow more light into the eye. This enlarging of the pupil happens to us automatically. Let's try to observe this process.
2. Ask one of the children to volunteer for the experiment. Identify the pupil as the dark center of the eye. Are all pupils the same size? Look at other children's pupils. Most will be about the same size.
3. Place the paper grocery bag over the child's head and wait a minute for the pupil to open.
4. Quickly lift the bag off and observe the eye. A larger pupil should be observed; the size will quickly become smaller, so watch carefully. Try this with several children and let the children try it with their friends. They can also watch their own eyes in a mirror.
5. Conclusions to be drawn from this experiment are that the brighter the light, the smaller the pupil will become; the darker the environment, the wider the pupil will become.

Want to do more?

Cats and dogs have the same kind of pupil contraction. The children may be able to observe this in their pets by taking them from a dark place to a light place. Observe eye pupils in a dark room.

Language you can use

pupil
iris
contract
expand
light
dark
big
little
compare

Things you will need

a large paper grocery bag
mirror

Spot the Creeper—Peripheral Vision

Language you can use

vision
see
peripheral
field of vision
direct sight

Things you will need

chair
blocks to note vision boundary
optional—music

Peripheral vision is important for many jobs. Pilots and truck drivers need to be aware of the events taking place outside of the direct visual observations being made. Most sports use peripheral vision. What is peripheral vision? Can we learn to use it better? Let's find out.

What to do

1. In your discussion of sight and seeing, one of the traits of that sense which can be emphasized is the vision a person is able to use when not looking directly at an object. People can "see out of the corner of their eye" is an old saying that refers to our side vision.
2. Most of us should have about the same peripheral vision, and we can check this out through this activity. Ask one of the children to sit very straight in a chair and look ahead at a point at eye level.
3. About two meters (six feet) away, have a child creep into the field of vision of the watcher. This must be done silently or another sense will be used. You could also play "Creeping Music" to hide movement sounds.
4. When the child sees the creeper in her peripheral vision, she says, "Stop!" Place a block at this point.

5. Move in or out from that spot about a meter and repeat the creeping. The boundary of the vision should form a straight line away from the watcher.
6. Repeat this on the other side. The angle away from the watcher should be about the same for both eyes.
7. Try this with several children and note any variations.

Want to do more?

The "Blind Spot Card" can be introduced using these directions: On a 3 x 5 inch card place an X and an O about seven and a half centimeters (three inches) apart. Cover the left eye. Hold the card in the right hand so the X is on the left side. Have the children look at the X with the right eye and bring the card toward the eye. The O should disappear at the blind spot. Switch eyes if it works. This may be tough for little ones. It may help to make the X and O different colors.

I See You—Can You See Me?

Can you see someone's eyes in a mirror without the other person seeing your eyes in the mirror? This activity uses the eyes in discovering problems that involve the scientific processes of predicting and inferring.

What to do

1. Place the mirror flat against the wall at the eye level of the children.
2. Have one child stand back and to the right of the mirror.
3. Have this child predict where a partner must stand for the first child to see the partner's eyes. Have the partner move to the selected place.
3. Can the child see the partner's eyes? If not, try predicting another spot.
4. What happens if you or your partner move farther to the side? What happens if you move further back? Is there a spot where you can see your partner's eyes without your partner seeing your eyes?

Want to do more?

Experiment with different-sized mirrors. Children can work individually by predicting placement of objects.

> *I've seen you where you never were.*
> *And where you ne'er will be,*
> *And yet you in that very same place,*
> *May still be seen by me.*
>
> *(Reflection in a mirror)*

Language you can use

eyes
sight
reflect
mirror
right
left
move

Things you will need

small mirror

Phenakistoscope Creations:
Put the Bird in the Cage

Language you can use

motion picture
persistent vision

Things you will need

copies of the
drawings in the
illustration

crayons
index cards
pencils
stapler
stamps
stamp pad

Peculiar to the human eye is the phenomenon of "persistence of vision" in which the image of a subject remains with the eye for about one tenth of a second after viewing. This attribute allows the motion picture to be a reality. This can be demonstrated by swinging a flashlight in an arc through a darkened room. One can see the path of the light after the movement has been made. Your students can use this phenomenon to make their own motion picture device. The fancy name for this device is a phenakistoscope. Another persistent vision device is the thaumatrope. An easier word for that device is the flip book.

What to do

1. Make copies of the pictures in this activity. Attach them to index cards. Color one of the pictures; faintly outline the other. Staple the cards onto a pencil as shown in the illustration.
2. Rotate the pencil rapidly in the palm of your hand. Show the children how to do this.
3. Place the picture at eye level and rotate. The two pictures will appear in the "mind's eye" as one picture. The bird will be put in the cage.
4. Make up other cards with stamps. A dinosaur can land on the back of another, a bird can perch on a limb, a bug can land on a leaf, put an X in an O, dot the I...

Want to do more?

Make up flip books. Slow down a movie so the children can see the different frames move through their field of vision.

STAPLE
CARDS
BACK-
TO-BACK
ON EACH
SIDE OF
PENCIL

Winking and Blinking

Language you can use

communicate
wink
blink
signals

Things you will need

children

a series of eye signals you can use to communicate

We use our eyes for much of our nonverbal communication. As a part of growing up, children pick up those skills. Children learn when they can pass the "look" of a parent, and when not to. They learn that a twinkle in the eye counters a serious face and probably means something fun will happen. Eye communication is a very important skill that becomes even more highly skilled as one develops in a culture. It is a major means of sharing thoughts and feelings.

What to do

1. Talk about communication in general. Talking is one form of communication; writing is another. Can we talk with our eyes? Shall we try to make up a set of signals that can be used in the room to give directions without talking?
2. Make a list of the different eye movements that can be used. Winking or blinking can be used to tell numbers or answers, such as yes or no. Have the children create the commands and agree on their meaning. Practice the commands. Do head and eye movements together count or just eye movements?
3. Try the language out for a short time. What are the disadvantages of this type of language?

Want to do more?

Discuss how eye language can be improved. This may be the time to discuss what it would be like to be deaf and not be able to use communication based on sound. Talk about and try sign language.

Eye winker,
Tom tinker,
Nose dropper,
Mouth eater,
Chin-chopper, chin-chopper.

Blinking is a reflex action; each of us has his or her own blinking rate.

Listen Up: A World of Sounds

Listen Up: A World of Sounds

INFORMATION PLEASE

How do the ears work?

The sense of hearing, or the AUDITORY sense, is centered primarily in the ear. The ear detects and carries sound vibrations to the brain. When the sound vibration approaches the ear, it is channeled down the ear canal, or the OUTER EAR, to the EARDRUM. The eardrum is a thin membrane stretched over the ear passage. On the inside of the eardrum are three tiny bones that pass the vibrations to another thin membrane called the OVAL WINDOW. The tiniest bones in the body are these three. This window is the entrance to a liquid-filled chamber called the COCHLEA. Waves in this liquid cause nerve impulses to be sent to the brain through the AUDITORY NERVE, and we hear sounds. AUDITORY MEMORY comes into play here because we learn sounds and memorize them to be recalled later. Located adjacent to the cochlea are the SEMICIRCULAR CANALS that are important in controlling and feeling balance. A chamber that lies adjacent to and around the bones of the ear leads to the inside of the throat. This chamber is called the EUSTACHIAN TUBE and is important in equalizing pressure within the ear chambers. Anyone who has ridden in an airplane or scuba dived knows how the Eustachian tube can be used to clear the ears and lessen the pain that often accompanies a change in pressure brought about by landing or descending.

How do our ears stay healthy?

Care of the ears is important. A brown wax is secreted by the outer ear. This traps small objects and bacteria, keeping them from the eardrum. This wax can harden if not washed out regularly. Warm water will dissolve the wax, and it can be flushed out. Problems of the inner or middle ear are generally more serious and may require the attention of a doctor. Doctors who specialize in the ear, nose, and throat are OTORHINOLARYNGOLOGISTS.

Ear care ideas

1. Avoid exposing a child to loud noise. Researchers believe that certain noisy toys, allowed too close to the ear, may cause hearing loss.
2. Clean the ears regularly and gently, with either swabs or lubricating oils. Pediatricians occasionally discover such obstructive objects as jewelry, marbles, beads, and stones in the ears.
3. See the doctor immediately if a child complains of an earache. In the event of a middle-ear infection, give the prescribed antibiotic, as directed, until none is left.

4. Take the child for audiometer checks at least once every two years, preferably to a pediatric audiologist.

How can I tell if a child has a hearing loss?

There are many signals to look for, but here are a few:
- A child who consistently talks louder or softer than other children.
- A child who doesn't respond or turn around when you speak to him or her from behind.
- A child who asks you to repeat sentences.
- A child who appears to be listening, but still doesn't seem to understand you.
- A child whose speech is unintelligible and difficult to understand.

Highs and Lows

Loudness, pitch, and quality are three important characteristics of sound. This activity focuses on pitch. The pitch of sound is determined largely by the frequency of the sound wave. A high frequency sound (for example, one in which relatively many complete waves pass a single point quickly) is a high-pitched sound. Similarly, a low frequency wave is associated with a low-pitched sound. This activity lets the children use their ears and hands as they sort high sounds and low sounds by their pitch.

What to do

1. Tell the children that you are going to say or play some high and low sounds. As they listen, you want them to identify the high sounds and the low sounds.
2. Sounds all have pitch. Some pitches are high and some are low. When you hear a high pitch, put your hand high into the air. When you hear a low sound, put your hand down low near your knee.
3. Proceed by playing or making a variety of high- and low-pitched sounds. You will need to coach children initially; however, as they practice, they will become more successful.
4. Explain that musicians play both high and low sounds on their instruments. They know what sounds to make because they read music. Show the children picture cards depicting a musical staff with a clef sign and a low note, another with a high note.
5. Play or hum a high note—hold up the high note sign. Play or hum a low note—hold up the low note sign.
6. Practice as before—children will soon master sorting the high and low pitches, putting their hands up for a high pitch and down for a low pitch.

 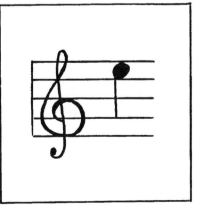

Language you can use

pitch
sound
high
low
voices
sign
symbol
high note
low notes
note
staff
music
frequency

Things you will need

talk in low and high voices (tape record, if you wish, a variety of voices both high and low)

drawings of a musical staff—one showing a high note at the top of the staff, and one showing a low note at the bottom of the staff

Want to do more?

Make musical instruments by stretching rubber bands crosswise over a shoe box. Pluck the strings. On another box, stretch another set of rubber bands lengthwise. Have children pluck the strings. What do you hear? Which has the high pitch? Which has the low pitch? Why? Experiment with glasses of water, filled and half-filled.

Eight percent of the population has some degree of hearing loss.

Little Sir Echo

Language you can use

echo
reflected
sound
bounce
delay
listen

Things you will need

Song "Little Sir Echo" by Laura R. Smith and J. Fearis. Sheet music 1917 by Bregman, Voco, and Conn, Inc. (J. Fearis and Bros.) or record of the song from "We All Live Together"

Echoes are reflected sounds. Sounds are reflected as they bounce off a distant wall, cliff, or other obstruction. This means we hear the same sound twice. In order for reflected sound to be heard as an echo, it must occur at least one-tenth of a second after the original sound. To hear an echo, we must be at least 17 meters (56 feet) away from the reflection surface. This concept of reflected sound is a bit too technical for young children; however, the word echo and what it represents can be imitated in the classroom. Take the children to a place where they can hear a real echo, if there is a place available.

What to do

1. Play record or sheet music while the children listen. An adult sings the song or plays the record and also does the echo part.
2. Explain what an echo is.
3. Sing the song again, showing the children when to sing the echo part.
4. Find a place where an echo can be made, such as a stairwell, a very large room, or a tunnel. These places may produce echoing sounds, but are not likely to produce a true echo.

Want to do more?

Let the children take turns being the leader and the echo. Tape record an echo for the children to hear.

"We All Live Together," Volume 1, Youngheart Music Educational Service, PO Box 27784, Los Angeles, CA 90027. Telephone: 213-663-3223

Find the Clock—Ear Detectives

This activity provides a means to use the ears in problem solving. By listening carefully, the children attempt to locate this source of sound that has been carefully hidden in the room. Hurry and find the clock before the alarm goes off and awakens the baby!

What to do

1. The baby has been put down to take a nap. Mother suddenly remembers that the alarm clock is set to ring in five minutes. She starts to search for the clock, but she can't find it anywhere. Let's help her search for it. Use your ears! Listen for a ticking sound. Hurry! Try to find it before the alarm goes off and awakens the baby.
2. The clock should be set and well hidden in the room. It does not have to be visible. However, it should be audible when the children get close to it.
3. If the alarm goes off before the clock is found, try it again.

Want to do more?

Add another clock.

Tick, tock, where's the clock?
Where did (teacher or
*   child's name) hide it?*
Quiet, listen for the sound,
Then we're sure to find it.

Language you can use

listen
quiet
search
look
find
sound
alarm
clock
ticking

Things you will need

winding alarm clock with an audible tick
doll

Noise Blockers

Language you can use

noise
sound
clock
ticking
muffle
block
blocker
insulation
sleep
awake

Things you will need

alarm clocks
cardboard boxes

a variety of insulating materials, for example, newspaper, straw, beans, rice, cloth

Have you ever gone to your grandparents' house, stayed overnight and slept in a room that has a loud ticking clock? Sometimes this sound can be relaxing, helping you to go to sleep. At other times, it can be annoying and will keep you awake. This activity lets children experiment with a variety of materials that can be used to muffle sounds. Which is the best noise blocker? When you find the answer, remember to take some to grandma's house the next time you visit.

What to do

1. Work with groups of four or five children.
2. Give each group a loud ticking alarm clock and a cardboard box.
3. Give each group a large quantity of insulating material.
4. Let the children predict which material they feel will be the best noise blocker.
5. The children begin packing and listening for the ticking sound to fade and finally disappear.
6. Which blocker was effective with the least amount of insulation?
7. Which noise blocker do you wish you could take to your grandma's house?

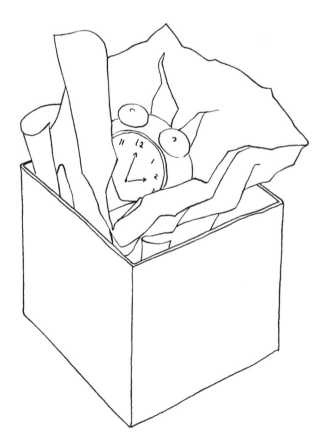

Want to do more?

Try the activity with a tape player, playing of course.

> *The Clock*
> *Tick, tock, tick, tock,*
> *Merrily sings the clock;*
> *It's time for work,*
> *It's time for play,*
> *So it sings throughout the day.*
> *Tick, tock, tick, tock,*
> *Merrily sings the clock.*

Using Our Ears at Home and School

Gross sound discrimination is a pre-reading skill. It provides much enjoyment for children as they sharpen their listening skills. It also helps prepare them for the finer sound discrimination needed for reading.

What to do

1. The teacher tape records short segments, 15 to 30 seconds, of a variety of sounds made in the home—dishes being washed, both hand and automatic dishwasher, radio, television, telephone, toilet flushing, washing machine, door being closed, opening window, etc.
2. Recordings should also be made of school sounds—playground noises, school bus pulling away, circle time, doors closing, and any other sounds specific to your school environment.
3. Play the recording, stopping after each segment. The children should attempt to identify the site of the sound—school or home. Also identify the sound source.

Want to do more?

Purchase a record or tape of sounds—available in record stores. These are professionally made and include a vast variety of gross sounds that can further sharpen gross sound discrimination skills. Prepare a sheet with a picture of each sound on the tape. The younger children can point to the object making the sound. Older children can draw a picture of the object making the sound.

Language you can use

listen
sound
ears
identify
where
which
think

Things you will need

tape recording of sounds common to households and schools

Tick Tock—How Close Is the Clock?

Language you can use

clock
close
far
distance
measure
record
compare
hear
listen
sound

Things you will need

a wind-up clock that has a clearly audible tick

masking tape
marker
paper
string
meter stick or ruler
paper and pen

Our ears are very sensitive to the sounds that are made in the world around us. How close does a sound maker have to be before we hear it? This depends upon the sound that is made. Is it loud or soft? Harsh or pleasant? This activity focuses on listening and measurement.

What to do

1. Have one child sit in a chair or on the floor with eyes closed or covered with hands.
2. Approach this child with the clock, walking slowly from a distance from which the ticking is inaudible.
3. Walk in a straight line toward the child.
4. The child is to say, "Stop," when the ticking is heard. Mark the stopping point with a piece of masking tape. Put the child's name on the tape. Repeat with several children, having one child be the walker and another the listener.
5. Use string, a meter stick, or a ruler to measure the distances.
6. Make a graph comparing various distances recorded.
7. Discuss how other sounds in the room, building, or outside affect how well we can hear. Can we find a quieter place to play this game?

Want to do more?

Do the same activity using a ticking wristwatch or an alarm beeping wristwatch. Compare the audibility distances of the two timepieces.

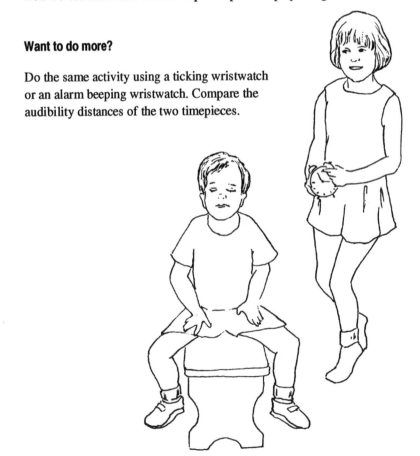

Water Sounds

Our ears hear sounds in the air. They can also hear sounds through water. This activity explores sound travel, as well as sound discrimination, in air and in water.

What to do

1. Fill the aquarium or jar 3/4 full with water.
2. Press an ear against the tank above water level. Now have a partner hit two spoons together inside the tank above the water. Listen.
3. Press an ear against the tank below the water level and listen as the spoons are hit again.
4. Now the partner hits the spoons together below the water level, while the child presses an ear against the tank below the water level.
5. Compare the sound above and below the water. Were they different? Do you think sound travels to our ears better in water or in air?

Want to do more?

Use other objects—pencils, rocks, blocks—and follow the same procedure. This really works well in the swimming pool.

Language you can use

hear
sound
travel
ear
fast
slow
identify
strike
hit

Things you will need

aquarium or
gallon glass jar

water
two spoons

It is not the sea you hear when you put a shell to your ear, but the sound of the blood flowing in your ear.

Auto Lotto

Language you
can use

match
listen
record
hear
lotto
game
cover
board
sounds

Car parts such as
door, window,
hood, brake,
trunk, radio, mu-
sic, horn, direc-
tional signals,
blower, wipers,
air in tire, key in
ignition, gear

Things you will
need

tape recorder
car
cardboard
squares

precut pictures
of auto sound
sources—these
can be obtained
from a car dealer
or auto maga-
zines

Lotto is an old familiar game that can be used to sharpen acuity skills as children identify familiar sound sources. Let the children help gather the sounds
for this activity. They can also assist in making the game cards.

What to do

1. Take the children to your car (or a parent's or volunteer's car).
2. Discuss the many sounds that we can hear from one sound source—the car.
3. Ask the children what sounds they think the car makes?
4. Record the sounds made by various parts of the car. Sounds should be recorded separately. Some suggestions are door closing, door opening, hood
raising, hood closing, horn sounding, engine starting, engine stopping, trunk
opening, trunk closing, radio playing, directional signals clicking, heater or
air conditioner blowing, putting air in the tire, turning key in ignition.
5. Prepare game cards. You will need two pictures of each sound source. Use
one picture to make game boards of four pictures of car parts that are sound
sources. Use the second picture of these same sound sources to make individual matching auto sound cards to cover the game boards.
6. Play the tape. Use fast forward and reverse if you want to vary the order in
which the sounds are heard. Play only a short segment of each.

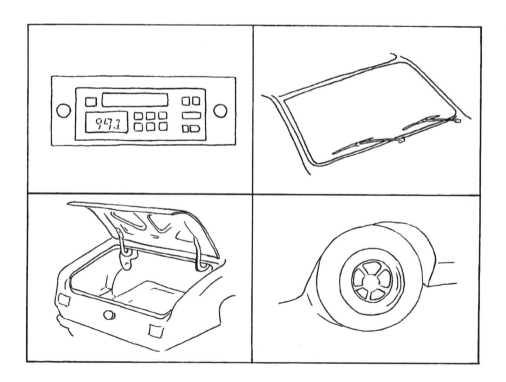

7. The children listen, identify the sound, and cover it with a matching sound card if it is on their game board.
8. Keep playing until all the sounds have been identified and all game boards are covered.

Want to do more?

Do the same activity using animal sounds, classroom sounds, or some other source.

Mystery Child of the Day

We use our ears to hear sounds that are made by people, animals, and moving objects. This activity focuses on the unique sounds that are made by our voices as we talk to each other. It emphasizes the uniqueness of each person. Your voice is your very own sound and only you can make it. Be sure to play back the recording too.

What to do

1. Briefly tape record an interview with each child. Interview questions can focus on any topic—favorite foods, pets, games, colors. Names of the interviewees are not revealed.
2. Play the recording of one interview for the class.
3. Ask the children to identify the child by name.
4. Emphasize that many voices are similar in sound; however, by listening closely we will find that the mystery voice gives us clues that will help us to identity him or her. What are these clues? Listen carefully and find out.

Want to do more?

Interview a significant adult in your school, such as the janitor, cook, principal, director, or other teachers. Can the children identify them by their voices? Have all the children repeat the same sequence of letters or names, or answers to questions (for example, How old are you? I am three years old.). Play these responses back. It will require even finer voice sound discrimination skills to identify the voices. Can they disguise their voices so others cannot recognize them? Use the tapes in a listening center—children can repeat this activity as often as they wish.

Language you can use

tape recorder
listen
identify
voices

Things you will need

tape recorder
blank tape

High and Low, How Do You Know?

Language you can use

pitch
high
low
listen
strike
hit
tap
identify

Things you will need

9 x 12 inch cards with high and low pitch symbols (see illustration)

a full and an empty ketchup bottle

wooden mallet or spoon

objects to strike, such as bells, chimes, tuning fork, pans, a striker, glasses

Pitch is a quality of sound; any produced sound can be classified as having the characteristics of a high or low pitch. This activity involves action and careful listening.

What to do

1. Talk about high and low sounds.
2. Give some examples of high and low sounds. Strike an empty ketchup bottle and strike a full ketchup bottle. Which sounds the highest, the lowest? Which has the highest pitch? The lowest pitch?
3. Strike a number of items. If the children think the sound is low-pitched, they hold up the low card. If they think it is high-pitched, they hold up the high card.
4. Proceed, striking other items you have brought in for the activity.

Want to do more?

Follow the above procedure, only strike items that are fixtures in your room— blocks, cabinets, tables, window, door, floor, etc.

Secret Sounds: How Well Do You Remember?

The ability for children to remember sounds is very important to their reading. Children with poor auditory memory are likely to be poor readers. Poor auditory memory may be tied to sounds of certain pitch or intensity that one can discover in this sound classification activity.

What to do

1. Place the children in a circle on the floor.
2. Bring out the sound-making objects; make the sounds. Have the children memorize the sounds and the sound makers. Go through the entire set.
3. Have the children lie down, hiding their eyes.
4. Select one object, make the sound. "Don't tell, I'll do it again."
5. Have the children sit up. Point to the objects sequentially. Can the children guess the correct sound maker?
6. Continue with the other objects.
7. Repeat the ones they have difficulty identifying. Notice individual children who are having difficulty.
8. Repeat the activity the next day. Add one new sound. Can the children identify this new sound?

Want to do more?

To test auditory discrimination individually, select objects that sound very much alike. Put the objects at the back of the room for children to practice hearing.

Language you can use

remember
sounds
memory
auditory
names of sound objects

Things you will need

objects that will make identifiable sounds (five to begin) and more to add

Dear Deer Ears

Language you can use

external
ears
auditory
hear
amplify

Things you will need

pictures of animals with large external ears, such as a deer, an elephant, a dog, and a rabbit

The ears are a primary sense organ. Young children are not ready to deal with the inner workings of the ear, but they can begin to understand the function of the outer ear. By enlarging the outer ear with "deer ears," children can begin to understand that large animal ears aren't just decorative. Large ears help animals hear more than we can hear. If we "borrow" their ear design, can we hear more sounds?

What to do

1. Point to your ears. Ask the children to observe the ears. Talk about their shape and size. What is the purpose of the external ear? The ear part that allows us to hear is inside the head. The purpose of our outer ear is to funnel sound to the inner parts.
2. Examine pictures of animals with large ears. Compare these to human ears. How do they differ? Ask the children to describe the difference.
3. How can we make our ears hear better? One way is to enlarge our external ears. Want to try some special ears?

4. Roll the paper and cut as shown in the illustration.
5. Place the rolled paper in the forward position and take a hearing walk. Try to find some soft sounds to hear and amplify.
6. Rotate the deer ears to other positions. Take them on and off to compare what is heard.

Want to do more?

Make bigger ears. When you want to hear better, form "deer ears" with cupped hands. See eye activities for "amplifying" vision. How can you amplify your voice?

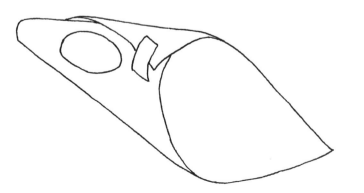

Dear, dear, deer ears,
Tell me what do you hear?
Little birds you can't see,
Or squirrels climbing in the tree?

Smart Ears

3

Our ears are sense organs that enable us to hear sounds. We use our eyes, as well as our ears, to identify the source of a sound. This activity explores the ability of the ear to hear and identify the source of sound without looking.

What to do

1. Talk about how we hear sounds, then look to identify the source. Give examples such as airplanes, honking horns, or birds.
2. We also use our ears to identify sound makers when we can't see them.
3. Place one object from each pair in front of one child.
4. Let the child examine each object. The matching objects remain in separate bags, or other suitable containers, that are not visible.
5. A second child, or the teacher, places an object (from one of the bags) in the shoe box. The first child should not know what it is.
6. The first child slowly tips the shoe box and listens carefully to the sound, then points to the object that he or she thinks is making the sound in the shoe box.
7. The second child opens the box. Does the object match or not? Switch roles and try it again.
8. What objects are the hardest to identify? The easiest?

Want to do more?

Add two objects to the box. Can you identify two at one time?

Language you can use

hear
taste
pair
identify
listen
choose
pick
sound
ear
place
tip
shake
open

Things you will need

shoe box

pair of each of the following objects: crayons, bottle caps, checkers, paper clips, marbles, ping-pong balls, buttons, etc.— some should slide, some should roll

one bag for each pair of objects

Name That Tune

Language you can use

listen
name
music
tune
identify
hear
ear
quickly
hurry

Things you will need

15-second recorded excerpts of music selections that the children are familiar with, for example, "Rock A Bye Baby," "Baa Baa Black Sheep," "Old MacDonald Has A Farm," "The Hokey Pokey," "Pop Goes the Weasel," etc.

hand bells

Children can learn to use their ears discriminately at a very early age. This activity requires careful listening, as only small segments of tunes are played. The children must listen carefully, then name the tune as quickly as possible. Reaction time, auditory perception, and memory all get a workout in "Name That Tune."

What to do

1. Explain that you will be playing some songs on the tape recorder. Two children will play at one time for each song. Each child holds one hand bell.
2. The two children use their ears to listen carefully as the song is played.
3. When one child thinks she knows what the song is, she rings the bell as fast as she can. The first one to ring the bell gets the first chance to identify the tune. If the first person gets an incorrect answer, the second player gets a chance.
4. If the tune isn't identified, rewind and let them try again. If there is still no answer, turn to the rest of group for help.
5. Now choose two more players.

Want to do more?

With younger children, do this as a whole group activity. Do the same activity with voices of teachers and other staff members at your school.

One or Two or Three, I Can Hear as Well as I Can See

Building good auditory memory is an important early learning task. Remembering sounds and the implements that make these sounds is a good beginning. Extra auditory memory activities can be built on volume and number of sound makers. This activity looks at numbers of sounds and asks children to distinguish those numbers.

What to do

1. Place three children in a line, one facing away and two facing front.
2. Give the three children the three pairs of sand blocks. Tell the three children that they are to play one, two, or all three sets of blocks.
3. A fourth child closes his eyes and tries to determine how many sets of blocks are being played.
4. Take turns until all the children have had a chance to play. Four tries is a turn.
5. Record the number of successes at each number made.
6. Add more kids to the circle. Children can discriminate how background sound effects hearing.
7. Play background music or sounds to disrupt the hearing. Discuss how background sound affects hearing.

Want to do more?

Clickers of ball point pens are soft sounds; put a hand over one ear to determine whether two ears are better than one.

Merry are the bells, and merry do they ring;
Merry was myself, and merry could I sing;
With a merry ding-dong, happy, gay and free,
And a merry sing-song, happy let us be!

Waddle goes your gait, and hollow are your hose;
Noddle goes your pate, and purple is your nose;
Merry is your sing-song, happy, gay, and free,
With a merry ding-dong, happy let us be!

Merry have we met, and merry have we been;
Merry let us part, and merry meet again;
With our merry sing-song, happy, gay, and free,
And a merry ding-dong, happy let us be!

Language you can use

count
distinguish
sounds
one
two
three

Things you will need

three pairs of rhythm band sand blocks

paper and marker
recorded music

Two or One, Which Is Better?

Language you can use

ear
plug
cotton
listen
both
one
two
hear
sound
raise
stand
measure
distance
blindfold

Things you will need

cotton

loudly ticking alarm clock

ball of string
scissors
blindfold
watch or timer
paper and marker

We hear best when we are able to make use of both ears. It's much easier to locate a sound source when both of the ears are listening. This activity proves this point.

What to do

1. Discuss the need for using both ears as we listen for sounds. When we use both ears, we can hear better.
2. Select one child and blindfold him. Place cotton firmly in one of his ears to block out the sound waves.
3. Take him out of the room. Have him wait outside until you call him in.
4. Hide a loudly ticking alarm clock somewhere in the room.
5. Bring the child back into the room. Instruct him to listen carefully with one ear and try to locate the clock.
6. Keep time and record how long it takes to find the ticking clock.
7. Repeat the activity with the same child, only this time no ear plug is used.
8. Compare the time it takes to find the clock with one ear and with two ears. Is it harder or easier to locate the sound with one ear?
9. Let other children try, following the same procedure.

Want to do more?

Do the ear enhancer activity—compare time used in sound location to the above.

A diller, a dollar,
A ten o'clock scholar,
What makes you come so soon?
You used to come at ten o'clock,
But now you come at noon.

Two Ears Are Not to Error—
Circle Time Sound Play

Our ears not only allow us to hear, but they help us locate the direction from which sound comes. Luckily we, and most other creatures, have two ears to assist us. The sounds that enter the ears are recorded twice in the brain. We automatically compare the information from both ears to determine location and distance. Are we as accurate with only one ear? Let's find out.

What to do

1. Have a child sit in the center of the circle during circle time, with eyes closed or covered.
2. Have one of the children in the circle strike the rhythm sticks.
3. The child in the center points in the direction of the sound source. The teacher or another child records whether the response is correct or not. Repeat with several other children. The point of recording the responses is not to emphasize who is accurate and who isn't. It is to determine roughly how accurate the group is when using both ears.
4. Repeat the above procedure with a hand held tightly over one ear. Record the results. Is there a difference?

Want to do more?

Use other objects to make sounds. Compare right ear and left ear accuracy. Make a graph of the results.

NOTE: You may want to have a child who is repeatedly unsuccessful evaluated for possible hearing loss.

Language you can use

hear
error
direction
record
ear
listen

Things you will need

two rhythm sticks

paper and marker for recording results

optional—blindfold

Your Nose Knows: It's More Than a Smeller Teller

Your Nose Knows: It's More Than a Smeller Teller

INFORMATION PLEASE

How does the nose smell odors?

The sense of smell is the most easily tired of the senses; however, human sensitivity to smell is much greater than taste. The OLFACTORY sense, as smell is known, is chemically activated and is very similar to taste in its action. For a substance to be smelled, it must first be dissolved in the liquid found near the nerve cells in the nose. A person with blocked nasal passages from a cold will not be able to taste food well because taste and smell are coordinated senses and complement each other. Several million olfactory receptors are found in the nasal passages and are associated with mucus-secreting membranes lining the upper nasal cavity. The receptors are specialized cells that are connected together to form the OLFACTORY NERVE that connects directly to the brain.

What is the sense of smell?

The sense of smell is the least understood of the senses, and it may be as complicated as the sense of sight. The sense of smell may be 10,000 times more sensitive than taste because so many more and varied kinds of receptors exist for smell. Smell is also unique because it has the only sensory nerves that are replaced or wear out at regular intervals of 30-45 days. Young children are less sensitive to bad smells, but learn to dislike them as they grow older. Smells are culturally specific. Scientists are finding many new things about smell in humans. They are finding that each of us has a "unique odor print" that can be as individualistic as a fingerprint. Some of us are born with smell deficiencies. Some of these are smell blindness and smell confusion. Our smell sense also declines as we grow old.

Besides housing the sense of smell, the nose has several other functions. It acts as a filter for the air you breathe by trapping dust and small particles in the little hairs that line the NASAL PASSAGE. Under normal conditions, each of us breathes from 16-24 times per minute. Air enters through the NOSTRILS that lead into the NASAL CAVITY. A sheet of cartilage called the NASAL SEPTUM divides the nasal cavity into the right and left side. The nose also warms the air passing into the lungs. That is why you should encourage children who are outside in the extreme cold to breathe through the nose rather than the mouth. When you blink, tear fluid leaves the eyes through a canal that goes into the nose. Tears and runny noses go together. SINUSES, the hollow spaces in the head, all empty into the nose. When the nose is blocked from a cold, these sinuses do not drain easily. Colds and runny noses are related. Problems associated with a cold are found in the nose and the ears. The same doctors that treat the ears are also experts in the nose. Doctors who specialize in the ear, nose, and throat are OTORHINOLARYNGOLOGISTS.

A sneeze can travel 100 miles per hour, the speed of a hurricane.

Bet You Can't Hold Your Breath Forever

Language you can use

inhale
exhale
breath
hold
time in seconds

Things you will need

paper and pencil
timer in seconds

The nose is the external opening for the respiratory system. This is the system that provides oxygen to the body for use in burning food and providing energy. The nose is also the exit for the gases that are produced by the body while using food. The primary gas that is emitted through the nose is carbon dioxide. Another by-product emission of the nose is water vapor. While the use and production of these gases is beyond the comprehension of the younger children, they do know that we breathe in and out, inhale and exhale. Breathing is an active process and can be counted and explored. This activity focuses on a portion of the breathing process called "holding your breath." How long will you last?

What to do

1. Talk about breathing and what it does. To the extent of the children's ability, discuss respiration and what it is. Describe the breathing activity. Identify inhaling and exhaling. Show how to hold your breath. Ask the children if they ever need to hold their breath. This is an important skill for swimming. Can you find more uses for holding your breath?

2. You will stop holding your breath when too much carbon dioxide is in your lungs. Our brain tells us to breathe, and we cannot stop the process. Some of us can hold our breath for a long time. We can practice holding our breath and become better breath holders.

3. Demonstrate how to hold your breath, and note the time your breath is held.

4. Ask the children to hold their breath while you time them individually. Note the time for each child on the data table. Be aware of children with asthma or other respiratory problems because they will not be able to hold their breath for long.

Want to do more?

Group the breath times. Find the longest, the shortest, the most common time. Do adults have a longer time? Bring in a swimmer or diver, time them. Find pictures of some animals such as the whale or seal who hold their breath for a very long time. What is the longest time a human can hold his or her breath? Pearl divers can hold their breath for several minutes. Compare that to the children's times.

Nose Talk

Language you can use

talk
vocal cords
expel
breath
communication
nose
air

Things you will need

children
paper and pencil

Much of the communication that takes place in the animal world uses sounds. Most of those sounds are created by the expulsion of air from the lungs through either the mouth or the nose. When we talk we expel air through the mouth and over the voice box where sounds are made. Most animals use a system similar to the human model, but some animals use the nose to communicate. One of those animals is the elephant, who trumpets to show feelings. We humans use our vocal cords for most of our communication, but we also use the nose. We will try with this lesson to look at the nose as a way to talk and see why the vocal cords are so much better.

What to do

1. Choose a day when runny noses are not prevalent.
2. Begin the class with a series of nose "blowings" that will try to communicate a request by the teacher. Try to duplicate crying, and ask the children what you are doing. Try sad nose sounds, other sounds.
3. Talk about how most of the ways we communicate with each other are through talking or using our eyes, but that we can develop other ways of communication if we know and agree on what the sounds mean. We can use our noses to talk about some things. Try different ideas suggested by the children.
4. Now have the children develop a way to "talk" to each other, using only the nose. Make it simple. For the rest of the time, the children can use only that language to ask for things or give directions. For example, at snack, two sniffs mean yes and one sniff means no.
5. Write down the language so you can use it later or with other direction-giving activities.

Want to do more?

Try the communication activities in the other sections. Which sense organ is the most adaptable to communication? Find some animals that use the nose most in communication.

It's a pig.
—Christa, 4

Zoo Noses

Do you want something to do when the children are on a zoo visit? Noses of all those strange animals may be a good focus. All zoo visitors are, at one time or another, astonished with the variety, length, and use of the noses of various animals. How can we classify and categorize all of those strange noses? What will we learn in the process?

What to do

1. Show the children pictures of zoo animals that they will probably see on their zoo visit. Try to find pictures of all kinds of animals and include some that will have no visible nose. Fish, insects, spiders, crustaceans, and lower animals are examples.
2. Talk about what the nose is used for and how it attaches to the lungs so we can breathe in air and use the oxygen from the air in our bodies. Many of the animals we will see in the zoo breathe air as we do.
3. Pass out the pictures and have each of the children determine whether the animal has a nose, then find the place on the picture where the nose is located.
4. Pass the pictures around so the children can observe what their classmates have found.
5. With the children, develop a statement about the location of the nose on the bodies of most zoo animals. That statement will say that the nose is found on the head and usually at the anterior tip—front end—of the body. Finding the nose of most lower animals will be difficult. Fish and sharks have gills; you can locate the gill openings on the sides of the heads. Insects and other crustaceans have air openings on the sides of the abdomens.
6. Go to the zoo and do a search for noses. What do all those noses do? Ask the children to dictate their observations. What do we know about noses now?

Want to do more?

Visit the pet store. Write down observations on noses by length, size, color, and other variations. Do animals that feed a certain way have differently shaped noses? Create a nose collage.

> *The world is full of noses.*
> *Some big, some long, some small.*
> *Look for a nose on an ant,*
> *And you will find nothing at all.*
>
> *An elephant's nose is longer,*
> *Than any other you'll see.*
> *It's a nose that's right for an elephant,*
> *I'm glad it's not on me.*

Language you can use

nose
classify
group
similar
different
long
short
strange

Things you will need

pictures of zoo animals

paper to write down characteristics or note observations

Nose Shadows—Which Are You? Turned-up or Turned-down?

Language you can use

genes
turned-up
turned-down
nose
parents
shadows
project
record
trace
cut
profile

Things you will need

a darkened room

a flashlight or
any other light
source to project
a shadow

pencil
paper
scissors
paste

We are all individuals, different but similar in many ways. Over forty thousand genes are needed to make the recipe that ends up being you. There are numerous variations of this recipe. These variations are called traits and some show up more than others. This activity focuses on a variation outside of your body—your face, specifically your nose.

What to do

1. Discuss dominant and recessive traits, and how we inherit these from our parents. Some traits are dominant and some are recessive. This means if you inherit a gene for a turned-up nose from one parent and a turned-down nose from the other, chances are good that you will end up with a turned-up nose because the turned-up nose is dominant.
2. Project face profile shadows on the wall using the projector or a flashlight.
3. Teacher traces the outline of the profile, carefully tracing the nose.
4. Children in class record the shape of the nose on a new graph.
5. How many do we have of each shape?
6. Let the children cut their profiles from the outlines.
7. Paste on paper and take home.
8. Discuss other dominant and recessive traits. Observe and record these in the same manner, only eliminate the shadow profiles.

Want to do more?

Examine other traits—dark hair (dominant), light hair (recessive), red hair (dominant); long eyelashes (dominant); dimples (dominant); bushy eyebrows (dominant).

Whose Nose Is Whose?

Do you think you could recognize some of your favorite book and television characters if you only saw their noses? This activity lets us discover that, although noses come in many shapes, sizes, and colors, we can't be fooled when it comes to learning whose nose is whose.

What to do

1. Paste pictures of famous characters in various pie portions of the paper plate. Pictures have noses covered.
2. Cut a window in the center of the paper plate (see illustration).
3. As children watch, put one of the famous character noses in the window.
4. Whose famous nose do you think this one is?
5. The children guess by calling a character's name. Keep a tally sheet of choices.
6. Lift the cover of the nose on the wedge. Is it a match or not?

Want to do more?

Make a famous nose college. Make nose matching cards so children could do this activity alone or in pairs. Make individual nose booklets.

Language you can use

famous
character
book
television
viewing
identify
think

Things you will need

paper plate
tally sheet
pen

pictures of noses cut from magazines, also the noses of Piggy, Kermit, Pinnochio, Dumbo, Bambi, Big Bird

How Smart Is Your Nose: Real vs. Artificial Smells

Language you can use

artificial
real
substitute
smell
scent
odor
match
observe
compare
similar

Things you will need

chewy candy in a variety of flavors—banana, strawberry, watermelon, mint, cinnamon or chewing gum with the same flavors

fresh cubes of watermelon, strawberries, a mint leaf, a banana, a cinnamon stick
small containers

When is something real? When is it artificial? Some things that are artificial are made to look, taste, and smell just like the real things. This activity reveals just how good candy and gum manufacturers are at this process. It also lets the children use their noses in a scientific activity by observing and comparing.

What to do

1. Explain that artificial flavors are used in candy and gum. These flavors are made of chemicals that are mixed until they smell and taste very much like the actual item they are attempting to duplicate.
2. Put candy and gum (artificially flavored items) in the containers. Use a separate container for each item.
3. Follow the same procedure for the real items.
4. Have the children open the jars and match by smell the real to the artificial items (for example, banana candy smell to actual piece of banana, mint gum smell to actual mint leaf).

Want to do more?

Use Kool Aid or Jell-O in the same manner.

Popcorn Hunt

The sense of smell always gets a workout when we pop popcorn. The smell of the popping kernels of corn permeates the house or the school building. This activity shows how the sense of smell is stimulated by cooking odors of one of many children's favorite foods, popcorn.

What to do

1. Tell the children to try to find the popcorn. It's not popped yet. Have it well hidden in the room. The hidden amount should be enough for one popper full.
2. Give them clues as they get near the popcorn. You're getting warmer, colder, etc.
3. Pop the popcorn in another room in the building. Ask the children to find the popcorn now. There will be no clues given. You must use your nose, your sense of smell, to find it.
4. When the children locate the popcorn, let them eat it as a snack.
5. Compare popcorn smells, popped and unpopped. Compare popcorn texture, popped and unpopped. Compare popcorn color, popped and unpopped.

Want to do more?

Measure the amount of unpopped corn and compare to the same amount popped. Do the same activity with fresh baked bread, pizza, cookies, and other favorites.

Language you can use

kernels
popcorn
cook
find
seek
smell
scent
odor

Things you will need

popcorn popper
heat source
popcorn
oil

Scratch and Sniff

Language you can use

observe
group
classify

Things you will need

scratch and sniff stickers

index cards or paper squares

optional—crayons or pictures of the scent

Scratch and sniff stickers are available to most of us and can be used by children to explore the sense of smell. They can identify strange and familiar odors, and we can discuss odors, using scratch and sniff stickers. The chemical industry has worked marvels to bond smells into pieces of paper so children can use them over and over. Now we'll use those stickers to help children to look at scratch and sniff through the eyes of a young scientist.

What to do

1. You will need 10-15 scratch and sniff scents. You may want to make up sets, so a few groups can do the activity.
2. Place a scent sticker on each index card or paper square. On the reverse side write the scent name or paste/draw a picture of the scent it professes to mimic.
3. Show the children how the scratch and sniff cards work.
4. Give the cards to three to five children, asking them to sort the piles into a good smelling and a bad smelling pile. Some of the children will not know what some of the scents are and/or will not be able to name them. That is fine. They can group without knowing the name.
5. Go through the set with each group, reviewing why they made the decisions they did. At this time, you might identify smells.

Want to do more?

Try other ways to classify the smells: strong/weak, food/not food, happy/sad. Match smells to real food; make pairs to be matched with eyes closed.

Searching for Hidden Treasure

4

This activity lets the children use their sense of smell and beginning map reading skills as they follow the clues to the hidden treasure.

What to do

1. Give the children a map of the playground or classroom. Mark the location of hidden smell jars on the map. An adult should accompany the children and interpret the map, if necessary. Explain to the children that they will be given small clues that will help them find the hidden treasure. The map could have smell stickers to match the hidden smell jars or hints such as, "this smell comes from something long and yellow."
2. Collect the clues as you follow the trail. Can the children identify the fruits?
3. Follow the trail of smells until you reach the end—the treasure box. Open it and share the fruit salad made with fruits found on the treasure hunt.
4. Examine the clues the children have collected. Can they find the same fruits in their salad?

Want to do more?

Can the children identify the fruits with eyes closed, using only their sense of smell? Group fruits by similar characteristics. Examine any seeds you can find.

Language you can use

treasure
trail
smell
clues
map
find
hidden
fruit names

Things you will need

small cubes of food items in small containers (apples, oranges, grapes, bananas, watermelon, pineapple, pears, cherry, etc.)

fruit salad for the group made from the fruits hidden for the hunt

large box or cooler decorated as a treasure chest

map of the playground or classroom

optional—smell stickers

Mobile Odors

Language you can use

odor
smell
travel
move
fast
slow
mobile
raise
hands
first
last
chart
olfactory
diffuse

Things you will need

small amount of ammonia in a pill bottle

a simple map of the classroom on a large sheet of paper

crayons

The sense of smell is located in the nose. The nerve endings in the nose, olfactory nodes, are sensitive to odors in the air. These odors diffuse through the air silently and unseen. This activity demonstrates how fast an odor can travel and lets the children map its path.

What to do

1. Ask the children to find a place to sit. Be sure that they are scattered throughout the room.
2. Tell them that they should put their hands up when they smell the ammonia. Do not raise them if they don't smell it. We want to find out how the smell travels.
3. Open the bottle.
4. Chart the path of the odor on the map as the children raise their hands.
5. What path did the smell take?

Want to do more?

Try a variety of smells. Do some smells travel farther or faster than others? Does it make a difference if the window is open or closed? Put a scent in a cabinet with the door closed. Is there an effect on how fast the smells travel?

Our sense of smell is poor compared to that of many animals, such as deer and dogs.

Scented Necklaces

When the nose smells the same odor for a long time, the nerve endings become deadened to that particular scent. This is especially obvious with strong odors.

What to do

1. Open the extract bottles one at a time. Can the children identify the smells? Don't they smell wonderful? Which smell do you like the best? Wouldn't it be nice to smell your favorite all the time?
2. Ask each child to choose a favorite smell. Put a SMALL amount of the chosen smell on a cotton ball and tie it with string to make a necklace. Before long, each child will have a favorite smell necklace.
3. After awhile, ask the children if they can still smell the necklace. Is the smell gone?
4. Take the necklaces off and tape each one to a card with the child's name. Go outside for awhile.
5. Smell your necklace when you come back in. What happens?

Want to do more?

How else can we rejuvenate our smellers? Go outside and breathe in fresh air with the necklace still on. Do some smells last longer than others? What happens if you splash water on your nose? If you smell a second smell for awhile, can you smell the first smell again?

Herb Detectives

Language you can use

herbs
cooking
smell
basil
chives
mint
oregano
parsley
rosemary
sage
thyme
compare
shape
texture
match

Things you will need

both fresh and dried herbs:
basil, thyme, rosemary, sage, parsley, oregano, mint, chives
zip lock bags

Do you ever get to help mom or dad cook? If you have, you have probably seen them put herbs into the food as it is being cooked. Herbs have unique smells as well as tastes. This activity helps children become familiar with a variety of herbs used in cooking. It also lets them compare fresh and dried herb smells.

What to do

1. Place the dried herbs in zip lock bags.
2. Discuss how herbs are used in cooking. Let the children share their experiences.
3. Show the herbs, giving special attention to their shape, texture, and smell.
4. Pass the zip lock bags around and let the children examine the herbs. Let the children handle and smell the fresh herbs. Compare these to the dried herbs.
4. After all herbs have been introduced, let the children work in pairs and try to match the dried ground herbs with the fresh herbs, using the sense of smell.

Want to do more?

Do the same activity, using the sense of taste to match. If fresh herbs are not available, use a variety of herbs purchased at a grocery store. Parents may be able to send fresh herbs from their gardens.

Mystery Noses—Nose Matching

All noses are beautiful! They come in many shapes, sizes, and colors. Yet many are very similar. This fun activity provides an opportunity to identify and match the characteristics of noses. It also lets us discover how very much alike we are.

What to do

1. Take close-up snapshots of each child's face.
2. After the film is developed, take each photograph and frame it with paper so that only the nose is visible (see illustration).
3. Do this activity at circle time. It's probably best to do only three or four mystery noses a day.
4. Show one of the framed pictures to the children.
5. Let them choose who they think the mystery nose belongs to. Keep a tally of the choices.
6. Now remove the frame—"It's Johnny!"

Want to do more?

Try mystery ears, feet, eyes, etc.

Language you can use

guess
mystery
looks
like
wonder
photography
frame
nose

Things you will need

construction paper
camera
film
scissors
tape
paper
pen

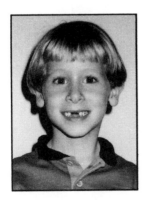
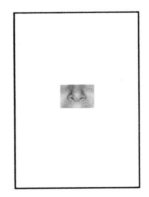

Molecules in My Nose*

**Language you
can use**

molecules
Jell-O
heat
boil
cool
solid
liquid
dissolve

The sense of smell is one that we use daily. One of the most frequent places this sense is used is in our kitchens at home. This activity explores the role that molecules play in the creation of odor. The children get into the act as they move from passive to extremely active molecules as the cooking odors gain in intensity.

**Things you will
need**

package of Jell-O
bowl
hot plate
pot for boiling
water
wooden spoon
Pyrex dish for
cooling

What to do

1. While seated around the teacher, have the children close their eyes. Hold up an unopened package of Jell-O. Can the children tell what it is? Can you smell what it is? What do you have to do to know what it is?
2. Have them open their eyes. Can you tell now? How can you tell what flavor it is (color on box, fruit shown)? Can you smell anything now?
3. Open and pour into a bowl. What can you smell now?
4. Talk about what it feels like to be cold or cool. What you might do (stay close together, huddle together). That is what molecules do.
5. Boil water and pour into the bowl. You may wish to note that the powder dissolves and is a liquid.
6. Talk about what happens when you begin to warm up (move apart, don't want to be too close to other things).
7. Have children move apart. Note the odors rising from the pot.
8. Then it gets hot, so hot in the pot that the molecules start to move and wiggle and jump to get away. Children begin to wiggle more and more.
9. As it gets hotter and hotter, the molecules move faster and faster and jump out of the pot to get away from the heat and move around the room. Children move about as molecules. And that is what happens to the Jell-O; the molecules jumped out of the pot and jumped into your nose. Cool the Jell-O and have it for a snack. Note it has turned into a solid.

Want to do more?

In cold weather, Jell-O can be cooled outdoors rather than in the refrigerator. Discuss other favorite foods their parents make, and how they can tell what they are even when they are not in the room. Note the smells as they occur throughout the year. Ask children to tell about molecules they find in their noses and report back. Be careful to warn parents. We wouldn't want them to think there was something up their children's nose (i.e., misunderstand molecules for marbles).

*Suggested by Barbara Goldenhersh

Happy Holiday Noses

Remember the old shake, listen, and match game. Let's use the same basic ideas to learn about the sense of smell and favorite holiday foods.

What to do

1. Discuss the smells of your selected holidays.
2. Place cotton absorbed with a specific scent in each canister. Prepare a pair of canisters for each scent. On the bottom of each jar put a picture of the scent item. For example, for Thanksgiving you might use cinnamon, cloves, pumpkin, sage, and cranberries.
3. Make cards that matching the scent pictures.
4. The child is to match the two containers, using the sense of smell, and find the identifying scent picture card.

What to do

Make fall and spring smell jars, make "My Favorite Smell" collections.

Language you can use

smell
scent
match
find
same
different
pair
alike
holiday names

Things you will need

baby food jars
cotton
scents associated with the holidays you have chosen

pictures of the items glued on cards

Nature Scent Sacks

Language you can use

walks
scents
odor
nature

Things you will need

small paper sacks
blindfold

collected items such as clover, wild onion, flowers, mint leaves, ginger roots, bark, moss, clover (items will give more distinct odors when broken or crushed)

The great outdoors has many special odors that we often don't take the time to enjoy. This activity combines a nature walk with a sense of smell activity that can be done when the children return back to the classroom.

What to do

1. Take a nature walk. Children can carry collecting bags and gather items with the teacher's supervision.
2. Upon returning to the room, sort the items and identify them with a lot of input from the children.
3. Have a separate sack for each collected item. Now place one item in each sack.
4. Blindfold one child.
5. Have another child hand this child a sack. Using only the sense of smell, the blindfolded child tries to guess what is in the bag.
6. Let the children take turns smelling the nature scent sacks.

Want to do more?

Add the sense of touch to this activity.

What do you smell?
What can it be?
If you use your nose
You won't have to see.

CHAPTER SIX

Open Wide and Say "Ahh": A Look Inside Your Mouth

Open Wide and Say "Ahh": A Look Inside Your Mouth

INFORMATION PLEASE

The mouth is the site of the sense of taste, the center of oral communication, the beginning of the digestive system, and one of the entry points for air into the respiratory system.

How does the sense of taste work?

The sense of taste, or the GUSTATORY sense is housed in the tongue. Lining the top and underside of the TONGUE and, to a lesser extent, the LARYNX (voice box) and PHARYNX (throat), are the TASTE BUDS. Taste buds are stimulated by only four basic sensations—bitter, sour, sweet, salty. Taste is a chemically based sense. A substance entering the mouth is dissolved in the saliva, resulting in a bathing of the taste buds, and taste results. The tasting area for bitter is found at the base of the lower part of the tongue. Sweetness is tasted at the tip of the tongue. Sour is found along the sides of the tongue while salty is found on both the tip and sides of the tongue. The senses of smell and taste are highly coordinated.

How do we talk?

Inside the mouth and at its far back where the throat begins is the LARYNX or voice box. The sounds we make to talk are produced there. The larynx contains VOCAL CORDS. As air is exhaled from the lungs it is forced past the vocal cords causing them to vibrate. This vibration causes sound. By regulating the amount of air flowing by and the tension on the cords, the sounds can be varied. Sounds are also moderated by the nasal and oral cavities before they pass out to be heard. Outer evidence of the larynx is the bulge found at the front of the neck. This area is called the ADAM'S APPLE.

How does digestion begin?

Digestion begins in the mouth where food is chewed and mixed with SALIVA (spit). Saliva contains an ENZYME that begins breaking down food so that it can be used in the body. Swallowing is a complex process that begins when the TONGUE and CHEEK push the food to the back of the THROAT. The throat muscles contract to push the food into the opening of the ESOPHAGUS. A small flap of tissue called the EPIGLOTTIS moves back and forth to open or close the airway to the lungs so food passes only into the esophagus. Most of us have had experiences with "food going down the wrong way," which means we have breathed in a small piece of food by accident past the epiglottis.

And what about teeth?

The teeth are important to digestion, appearance, and clear speech. PRIMARY TEETH, baby teeth, start arriving at about six months of age until 20 teeth are grown. Beginning about age six, children begin to loose these teeth. PERMANENT TEETH (32 in all) finally replace the baby teeth by pushing them out of the gums. There are four kinds of permanent teeth. The INCISORS are the four front teeth with flat edges used to cut food. The CUSPIDS or canines are pointed teeth found at the corners of the mouth and are used to tear food. The BICUSPIDS are just in back of the cuspids and are used to tear and crush food. The MOLARS are in the back of the mouth and are the main food grinders. The third molars found at the far back, called the WISDOM TEETH, are the last teeth to emerge. Teeth are embedded in the jaw bone. We see only the CROWN and the NECK of the tooth. The ROOT of the tooth lies in a socket in the jawbone. A hard, white, and pearly layer called ENAMEL covers the tooth. Enamel covers material called the DENTIN that surrounds the central or PULP cavity. In the pulp are found the nerves and blood vessels that make up the living part of the tooth. The pulp area is the site of all toothaches, as bacteria work their way through the enamel and dentin to infect the pulp. The American Dental Association and many toothpaste companies offer free and inexpensive materials on good dental hygiene.

What else is in the mouth?

Above the larynx is the PHARYNX. It is the connective tunnel that connects the mouth to the nose and respiratory/digestive tracts. TONSILS and ADENOIDS are projections into the pharynx that serve to capture and destroy bacteria. Healthy tonsils and adenoids are important to good health, but they can become inflamed and infected.

Feelings Are Fine

We all have different kinds of feelings. At times, we are happy, sad, frustrated, nervous, lonely, scared, proud, or angry. It can make us feel better when we share our feelings with others. This activity lets children express and share their feelings. Do this activity with a small group and introduce two or three feelings at a time.

What to do

1. Tell the children that it's okay to have different kinds of feelings. We all do.
2. Review the cards. The teacher should share experiences that might evoke such feelings. Share some actual experiences to model that it's all right to share feelings.
3. Shuffle the cards and place the deck face down.
4. Let the children take turns as they each choose a card.
5. Have each child enact a selected emotion. Make a similar face. Identify the emotion and share, if possible, situations the children have experienced when the emotion was felt.

Want to do more?

Let the children look at their faces in a mirror as they enact facial expressions. Let the other children try to guess what emotion is being expressed.

Language you can use

feelings
different
kinds
types
happy
sad
frustrated
nervous
lonely
scared
proud
angry

Things you will need

eight cards that have faces sketched on them depicting eight different facial expressions for feelings (see illustration)

Tongue Roll

Language you can use

inherit
trait
tongue
gene
genetic
parents

Things you will need

chart to record
observations
pen
mirrors

We often hear comments such as, "You look just like your dad," "You have your mother's eyes," or "Your grandfather's left-handed, too." Inherited tendencies are common. We look like our parents because we have received their genes. This lesson enables the children to see the path that traits take as they move from parents to child. Be sensitive to varying family structures as you present this activity to the children.

What to do

1. The tongue is a very important tool for talking, for swallowing, for eating, and for tasting. We don't often think of the tongue as an important organ, but it is. And it also is useful in telling us about our family.
2. Find two adults, one who can roll her tongue and one who can't. Have them demonstrate tongue rolling and the inability to roll the tongue. Those who can roll their tongues can both roll it and stick it out straight. Those who cannot roll their tongues are unable to do so no matter how hard they try. Being able to roll the tongue is not good or bad; it is simply a characteristic that is passed down from parent to child.
3. Find out what each of the children is able to do. Give each a mirror and have them determine whether they can roll their tongues or not. Make a chart with the child's name and the "kind of tongue."
4. Which condition is the most common? Some traits are called dominant because they appear most often or, when present in one parent, will overshadow the other parent's trait.

Who do I look like?
Some say my father!
But maybe, just maybe,
I'd rather look like my mother.

Want to do more?

Have each of the children go home to their parents and determine who can roll their tongue. Note these in a family chart and transfer to the class chart. Try eye color.

Pucker Power

The lips form the gateway to the mouth, a barrier to objects heading in and out, and a powerful muscle to do work when needed. This activity looks at the mouth in terms of its strong and highly flexible muscle called the Orbicularis oris or as it is more commonly known, the "puckerer."

What to do

1. Explain to the children that mouth prints are all different, just as fingerprints are. How could we make mouth prints?
2. Have the children classify the different ways they can shape their mouths. Smiling, frowning, yawning, kissing, and pouting are just a few.
3. Explain that we have a muscle, the Orbicularis oris, whose function is to control the shape of the mouth. Have your "O" muscle make a frown. What other shapes can your "O" muscle make?
4. One by one, put lipstick on the children with cotton swabs. Have each child choose a mouth shape and make a mouth print on a three by five inch index card. Identify the card with the child's name on the reverse side. Cover each print with clear tape to prevent smearing.
5. Every child will have a unique print and a unique shape to their lip print. When the prints are mixed up can the children find their own?

Want to do more?

Measure the prints. Make a collection on cards of all the different ways the mouth can be shaped and puckered by its muscle. Try to develop a way to classify mouth prints.

> *Says that little girl to the little boy,*
> *"What shall we do?"*
> *Says the little boy to the little girl,*
> *"I will kiss you."*

Only one bone in the head moves: your jawbone or mandible.

Language you can use

smile
frown
shape
print
oval
round
pucker

Things you will need

index cards
lipstick
cotton swabs
clear tape
marker

Big Teeth, Little Teeth: Coming and Going

Language you can use

baby teeth
deciduous teeth
permanent
adult
child
X-ray

Things you will need

X-rays of teeth

baby and adult teeth—replicas or real

We all have two sets of teeth. The first set grows to fit child-sized jaws. As we grow older, the entire body, including the jaw, gets bigger. Baby teeth fall out, and the adult teeth take their place in the full sized, adult jaw. Baby teeth are called deciduous teeth. This is the same name given to trees that lose their leaves every fall. It means falling. The second set of teeth are called permanent teeth.

What to do

1. Contact a dentist. Obtain X-rays of deciduous teeth with adult teeth showing in the jaw.
2. Make comparisons of adult teeth and baby teeth as the X-rays are examined.
3. Bring extracted baby teeth to school to examine. Make comparisons to an extracted adult tooth. Examine and compare size and root structure. The roots of the deciduous teeth dissolve to allow them to fall out and make room for the permanent teeth.

Want to do more?

Models of both types of teeth are available from a local dentist or dental society. Examine teeth from other animals.

When does a child have two sets of teeth? Just before the baby teeth fall out. The permanent teeth are hidden below the gums and force the baby teeth out.

How Many Pearlies?

Each of us has 20 baby teeth. Counting those teeth with a child helps us to focus on the dental care that will be important later. And the ability to recognize general shapes with real objects is important in developing spatial skills. The transfer of a sighting of teeth in a mirror to a visual impression or model on paper has important educational implications. So it is time to count and mark those baby teeth.

What to do

1. Give each of the children a picture of baby teeth and a mirror.
2. Discuss with them that most humans have 20 baby teeth at their age—ten on each jaw.
3. Each child is to use the mirror to determine if they have all their baby teeth. First note that we have two rows of teeth, upper and lower. Find these on the picture.
4. Teeth come in pairs, the two top middle ones are first. These are usually the first to fall out when children lose their baby teeth. Color these teeth in the picture.
5. The two teeth on each side of the top front teeth look alike. Color these in after they are found.
6. Go through all the teeth, one pair at a time, starting with the top row, then the bottom row.
7. Most children will have 20 teeth, unless they are at the teeth-losing age.

Want to do more?

Make clay imprints of teeth. Have a dentist come in or visit a dentist's office. Draw pictures of mouthfuls of teeth.

Language you can use

teeth
upper
lower
jaw

Things you will need

mirrors
children
drawings of baby teeth
crayons

This is my mouth filled with teeth which are all white.
—Alex, 4

Edible Toothbrushes

Language you can use

clean
brush
compare
classifying

Things you can use

food pictures
actual food items
from the list in
"What to do"

We all know that the best way to clean our teeth is by brushing them with a toothbrush and tooth paste. But did you know that some foods serve as self-cleaners for your teeth, while others do not clean but stick to your teeth and cause decay?

What to do

1. Some foods left in our mouths after eating are sticky, gooey sweets and acidic foods with sugar. These foods are bad news for your teeth. If you don't brush immediately after eating, bits of food left in your mouth are broken down by bacteria and produce acid. The acid attacks tooth enamel, eventually causing infection and decay.

2. By avoiding sticky, gooey foods and choosing self-cleaning foods, we help our teeth fight decay. Show and compare tooth attackers and tooth cleaners. Let the children compare and classify the following food items into tooth attackers and tooth cleaners.

- gum drops
- candy
- bread
- peanut butter
- raisins
- gum
- popcorn
- macaroni
- cookies
- carrots
- apples
- cauliflower
- celery
- melons
- tomatoes
- pickles

3. Emphasize that brushing is best—we can help our toothbrushes by avoiding the attackers—eat your dessert first.

Want to do more?

Have children plan snack menus using tooth cleaners as food items. Make picture books to take home of tooth attackers and tooth cleaners.

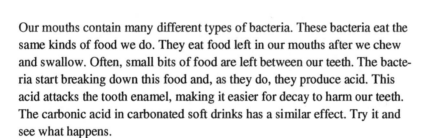

Mom makes me brush in the morning.
Dad makes me brush at night.
I don't always like to do either.
Sometimes I really fight.
When I'm older, though,
I'll know they both were really right.

More people have tooth decay than any other disease, but only one half of the kids 5-17 have tooth decay. Put your kids in the best half.

For One or Many

Our mouths contain many different types of bacteria. These bacteria eat the same kinds of food we do. They eat food left in our mouths after we chew and swallow. Often, small bits of food are left between our teeth. The bacteria start breaking down this food and, as they do, they produce acid. This acid attacks the tooth enamel, making it easier for decay to harm our teeth. The carbonic acid in carbonated soft drinks has a similar effect. Try it and see what happens.

What to do

1. Drop a baby tooth into a bottle of soda. Date the bottle.
2. Check the tooth once a week and return it to the bottle. Observe and discuss what happens to the tooth over a period.
2. To avoid the problem of decay, emphasize the need to brush teeth regularly. This will get rid of food, so bacteria can't have their lunch and leave their acids behind.

Want to do more?

Let an egg soak overnight in vinegar. Remove the egg and examine the shell. Since egg shells are similar in make-up and hardness to teeth, they both react to acid in similar ways.

Language you can use

bacteria
attack
decay
acid
brush
lunch

Things you will need

baby tooth
bottle of soda
label

Plaque Attack

When we don't brush our teeth regularly, they begin to feel dirty. It's as if something is covering them. Guess what? Something is! It's called plaque. Plaque is a mixture of food, saliva, and bacteria. At first plaque is soft and invisible. It builds up into a yellow, crusty substance called tarter. This eventually hardens on teeth, forming calculus, a substance that must be removed by a dental care professional. By using your toothbrush regularly, you can get rid of plaque before the bacteria start having lunch and begin to hurt your teeth.

What to do

1. Have all the children brush their teeth with toothpaste.
2. When brushing is complete, have each child chew a disclosing tablet. With young children, half a tablet or less may be enough.
3. Have them swish it around in their mouths for a few seconds and then rinse.
4. Look into the mirror. Red spots are plaque spots that you missed when you were brushing.
6. Review correct brushing technique.
7. Let children brush again and rinse.

Want to do more?

Contact the American Dental Society for brochures and posters.

Germs can't grow when they have nothing to eat.
Germs eat plaque. So brush plaque away!

The average child brushes 16 seconds. Dentists say brush for a minute. Add 45 seconds by using a timer.

> *Don't rush,*
> *Stop and brush.*
> *Love, Mom and Dad.*

Toothaches happen because bacteria in the mouth have eaten holes in the teeth. The ache happens when the nerve is exposed to the air.

Good Impressions

We can look at our teeth in many ways. Looking in the mirror is probably the most common way. This activity enables the children to get an even better look. We will make an impression and then a casting of teeth using plaster of Paris.

What to do

1. Do this activity with one child at a time, but in such a way that everyone can see. Make a clay mold that will fit into the child's upper mouth. Bite into the mold, pressing the clay tightly against the teeth to make a clear impression. Pull the mold carefully out of the mouth.
2. Repeat the process with another mold for the bottom teeth.
3. Wrap a strip of heavy foil around each mold and tape it in place. Mix plaster of Paris according to package directions. Pour the plaster of Paris into each mold. Be sure that it settles into the impressions by tapping the molds on the table.
4. When the plaster is dry, peel away the clay and foil. You should have good impressions of both the upper and lower teeth.

Want to do more?

Compare adult impressions to child impressions, looking at sizes and numbers of teeth. Have a dentist or dental hygienist come to supervise this activity. They can bring several sample impressions.

The Teeth
Thirty white horses upon a red hill,
Now they tramp, now they champ,
Now they stand still.

Language you can use

impression
mold
bite
pull
upper
bottom
teeth
tape
fill
plaster of Paris
stir
mix
thick
creamy
pour
set
dry
peel

Things you will need

plasticine—oil-based modeling clay

heavy-duty foil
tape
plaster of Paris
container for mixing plaster

Food Busters: First Steps in Digestion

Language you can use

digest
food
stomach
sugar
pour
broken up
powder
disappear
pieces
millions
tongue
taste
see

Things you will need

sugar cubes
empty glasses
wooden spoons
water

Our bodies use food in many ways. Some foods we eat make our bones strong and our teeth hard. Food also builds our muscles and keeps us warm. Before our bodies can do these things, they have to change the food we eat after we swallow it. Hamburgers and potatoes must be changed to liquids. Milk and juice, that are already liquids, have to be changed, too. This activity shows the children an example of how food is broken down into a liquid, the first step in the digestion process.

What to do
1. Use the above explanation of how food is used by our bodies.
2. Give each child two sugar cubes in an empty glass.
3. Break up cubes by crushing them with the wooden spoon. How do we crush the food we eat? We use our teeth.
4. After the cubes are broken up, fill the glass with water and stir until the sugar disappears.
5. Take a taste from the glass. Can you taste the sugar?
6. Where did it go? You can still taste it, but it has disappeared. It has dissolved into millions of pieces. We cannot see them, but our tongues can still taste them. In a similar way, the juices in our stomachs help break down the food we eat.

Want to do more?

Let the children dissolve a sugar cube in their mouths. Discuss how saliva provides the moisture to break down the cubes.

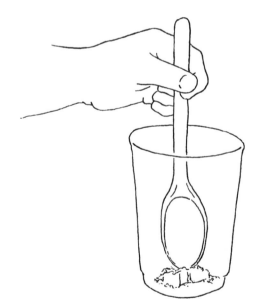

Upside-Down Swallow

What is involved in the act of swallowing? Let us dissect the practice and use the upside-down, impossible swallowing act as a way to encourage the children's inspection of part of digestion.

What to do

1. While you are having a snack, ask the children what it means to swallow. As they tell you what it means, ask the children to place a hand on their throat to feel the swallow. What does the tongue do when we swallow? Careful observation will indicate that muscles in the neck and mouth contract to allow the food to enter the alimentary canal.

2. Can we swallow upside down? Let's try. Ask a child to hang over a chair so her head is upside down. When she is stabilized, give her a cup of water to drink. What happens?

3. After the water has been cleaned up, talk about the way that gravity helps the muscles to do their job. The food actually falls down into the alimentary canal when it is forced through the entry in the throat.

Want to do more?

Try chewing a cracker upside down and swallowing. The shape of solid food will make it easier to have the muscles of the throat and tongue force it into the alimentary canal.

Food is moved down the throat by muscles, not gravity.

Some say you can stop hiccups by standing on your head.

> *Hiccup, snicup,*
> *Rise up, right up,*
> *Three drops in the cup*
> *Are good for the hiccup.*
>
> *Hiccup, hiccup, go away!*
> *Come again another day;*
> *Hiccup, hiccup, when I bake,*
> *I'll give to you a butter-cake.*

Language you can use

swallow
chew
gravity
masticate
digestion
alimentary canal

Things you will need

cups
water
chairs

3+

Spit

Most children are familiar with the word "spit." Spit is also called saliva. Saliva is a fluid used to help break down and digest food. Saliva comes from two small glands in the cheeks and under the tongue. The glands are called salivary glands. The saliva is released through little openings in the tongue. Digestion begins in our mouths. That's when we start breaking the food up into millions of tiny pieces. As we chew it, we break it up. This activity shows how both saliva and chewing breaks up our food before it is swallowed.

What to do

1. Give each child a piece of raw carrot and a paper plate or paper towel.
2. Ask the children to take a bite of the carrot and chew it eight times.
3. Spit it out onto the plate or towel. Observe the mixture.
4. Take another bite of carrot. Chew the carrot 20 times.
5. Now spit it out onto another part of the plate.
6. Observe the results. Is there a difference? What happens to food the more it is chewed?

Want to do more?

Do the same procedure with crackers.

Spitting Distance

Almost every child who has had a slice of watermelon has wanted to or has spit the seeds out across the lawn into the grass. Some schools have held spitting contests and have created graphs to note the huge distances that can be attained by those powerful "puckerers" from the kindergarten room. This activity is the advanced record keeping version of the spitting contests of old.

What to do

1. Discuss how the muscles of the body work and how the mouth muscle, along with the breath, can be used to propel seeds. Serve watermelon for snack. Give each child a cup or paper towel for saving the seeds.
NOTE: Young children should be carefully supervised to prevent choking.
2. Show them how to spit the seeds and allow them to practice.
3. Mark off a set of lines every 50 centimeters on a sidewalk or other flat surface. Include a zero or starting line. Take turns standing at line zero and spitting the seeds.
4. Have the children observe the way the seeds have landed. Note which is the farthest from the starting line and which is the nearest. Measure these to the nearest mark. Record these distances. Now note which distance is the most common. Are there several areas that have about the same amount, or do most of the children spit their seeds about the same distance? Scientists often use the term "average" to describe something most people do. How far did the average seed land in your group?
5. Try this again another day. Are the results about the same?

Language you can use

average
farthest
shortest
nearest
meter

Things you will need

watermelon

cups or paper towels

flat area with a line every 50 centimeters

paper and pen

Want to do more?

Try this with older kids or adults. Are the long spit and the short spit distances the same? Are most common distances the same?

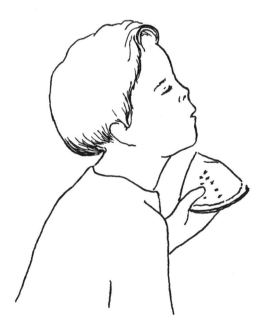

Umm, My Mouth's Watering

When we eat food, saliva is released into our mouths. What does it mean when someone says his or her mouth is watering? Sometime our mouths water when we only smell food. This is especially true with foods individuals find particularly appetizing.

What to do

1. Place the food in the butter tubs. Close the lids.
2. Discuss what saliva is, where it comes from, and how it works. You may want to refer to the "Spit" activity. Ask the children what kinds of foods make their mouths water.
3. Let's experiment with a few food smells and see what foods we have today that will make our mouths water. Be sure to emphasize that what makes Jimmy's mouth water may be different from what makes Sarah's mouth water.
4. Remove lids from tubs and pass them around for the children to sniff.
5. Ask what foods make your mouth water. Make a graph to make comparisons.

Want to do more?

Discuss how we like and dislike different foods. It's okay to be different.

Language you can use

smell
saliva
water
mouth
kinds
foods

Things you will need

paper and pen

3 food items that you feel will elicit a mouth-watering response from the children—popcorn, pizza, chocolates, mints, cookies, fried chicken, etc.

butter tubs with lids

Tasty Pairs

Foods come in a wide variety of forms. Many are processed by the time they reach the children's mouths. This activity focuses upon food sources and uses the sense of taste to discover "Tasty Pairs."

What to do

1. Show the children a variety of foods in their natural form—peanuts, apples, oranges, strawberries, potatoes.
2. Let them taste each of the foods.
3. Now discuss how foods are also eaten in other forms. They obtain other forms by being processed.
4. Show the children the processed forms of the above food items—peanut butter, applesauce, orange juice, strawberry jam, potato chips. Do not identify the original source.
5. Let them taste the processed food. See if they can match the "Tasty Pairs" correctly.

Want to do more?

Discuss how foods are processed. Visit a food processing plant. Process your own food by making something such as peanut butter or applesauce.

> *Simple Simon met a pieman,*
> *Going to the fair;*
> *Says Simple Simon to the pieman,*
> *"Let me taste your ware."*
>
> *Says the pieman to Simple Simon,*
> *"Show me first your penny."*
> *Says Simple Simon to the pieman,*
> *"Indeed I have not any."*
>
> *Simple Simon went a-fishing*
> *For to catch a whale;*
> *All the water he had got*
> *Was in his mother's pail!*

Language you can use

match
pairs
natural
processed
taste

Things you will need

peanuts, apples, oranges, strawberries, and potatoes in both whole and processed form

Working Together—Tasters and Smellers

Language you can use

cubes
sample
taste
tongue
smell
nose

Things you will need

small cubes of raw potatoes, pear, apple, and onion
small paper plates or napkins

Smell and taste are senses that work together to help our brains identify a substance. The substance must be in a solution or become dissolved in saliva to be tasted. If the surface of the tongue is wiped dry, some substances such as salt and sugar cannot be tasted. They have to be dissolved before they can be tasted. When we eat food, the two senses, tasting and smelling, work together to help us enjoy our foods. This activity demonstrates this interrelationship.

What to do

1. Have the children work in teams of two. One child closes his eyes. The other child presents food samples to be tasted.
2. The tasters should be given one sample at a time while holding their noses.
3. Can the tasters identify the food samples (raw potato, pear, apple, onion) by taste alone?
4. Repeat the activity. This time the tasters do not hold their noses. They do not taste the samples this time. They only smell them. Can the samples be identified by smell alone?
5. Repeat the activity, letting the children taste the foods without holding their noses. How well are the samples identified?

Want to do more?

Discuss why foods seem tasteless when suffering from a bad head cold or allergy.

Give Your Friend a Cold Game

The focus of this lesson is to share with the children the way that germs are spread through a sneeze. Because a germ transmission is an abstract concept, many of the younger children may not easily be able to transfer the sequence of germ to cold, and sneeze to germ to cold. But they can see the small drops in the air and possibly how a cold can be exchanged through a sneeze or cough.

What to do

1. Talk with the children about being very sick and having a cold. How did they feel when they were sick? Did they cough? Sneeze?
2. Explain that coughing and sneezing are ways that germs spread, causing colds in other persons. This game shows how that can happen.
3. Take a mister and spray it in the light. Fine drops of water will be suspended in the air and can be seen. Explain that when we have a cold, we sneeze and cough and spread germs in much the same way, especially when we do not put our hands over our mouths.
4. Rules for "Give Your Friend a Cold Game."

- Pin a piece of construction paper high over the chest (right side) of each child.
- Explain that you will spray one of them, giving that person the cold. To give the person a cold, the spray must show on the construction paper.
- When hit with the cold, the child becomes sick and moves to a "sick bay."
- When one child is sent to the sick bay, then one of the children already in the sick bay gets well and moves out to rejoin the group.
- The game is over when everyone has had a cold and made a trip to the sick bay.
- Review how colds are spread. The "mister" is a cough or sneeze. How could one prevent colds?

Want to do more?

Demonstrate how passing germs can be prevented by placing a cloth over the "mouth" of the mister during the game. Bring in masks worn by some people to prevent them from catching a cold.
To prevent the spread of germs:
1. Wash hands frequently and properly.
2. Keep the air fresh.
3. Don't crowd rooms.
4. Clean and sanitize all areas, toys and furniture.
5. Teach the children how to cough and sneeze correctly.
6. Keep personal items apart.
7. Require certain immunizations.

Language you can use

sneeze
cough
germs
cold
sick

Things you will need

plant mister or recycled window cleaner bottle full of water
pins
pieces of construction paper cut in 6 x 6 inch (15 x 15 cm) squares

A bleach solution that can be used to disinfect:

One tablespoon bleach and one liter (1 quart) of water

or
70 ml (1/4 C.) bleach and four liters (1 gallon) of water

Tongue Taste Test

Language you can use

taste
sweet
sour
salty
bitter
gustatory
observation
taste buds

Things you will need

cotton swabs
sugar water (sweet)

lemon water (sour)

tonic water containing quinine sulfate (bitter)

and salt water (salty)

The tongue helps us to eat as well as talk. It is also the site of our taste buds. These buds are hidden on the tiny bumps on the surface of the tongue. Taste buds contain the endings of nerve cells that send taste information to the brain. The tongue is assisted by our noses in sorting out various tastes through the sense of smell. The basic tastes are sweet, sour, salty and bitter. Salt is sensed at the tip of the tongue, sour on the sides, bitter at the base, and sweet under the tongue near the tip.

NOTE: When you plan an observation activity with tasting, familiarizing the children with chemical safety is a must.

What to do

1. Discuss what happens when you taste things, and how each of the children feel when certain fruits and foods are tasted. You could have some food for them to taste from each of the categories.
2. Tell the children that they can taste many things and identify them because they have memorized tastes, just as they have memorized the faces of their friends. But our mouths really only can tell four tastes or a combination of those four. Tiny pieces of the food we are eating find their way to a taste bud. This bud is like a tiny switch that tells our brains that we have eaten a certain food.
3. Have four children volunteer to begin the experiment. Mix up and label the solutions so you will know the contents: A=sweet, B=sour, C=salty, D=bitter.
4. Have the four children stick out their tongues and keep them out. Place a cotton swab in each of the solutions and then place only A on the first child's tongue tip (right at the end). Continue by placing B on the second child's tongue tip, and on to D. Ask the children not to swish their tongues around inside their mouth. The child with salt (C) should have tasted the salt, and the others should have had no taste until the solutions entered and joined the saliva to be disbursed through the mouth.
5. Try this with other children to show that most children will taste salt on the tips of their tongues.

Want to do more?

Continue through the set of tastes. Sweet is tasted over a far greater region than the other tastes are. Classify common foods by their taste. Which do you think is the best taste, the worst?

10,000 taste buds are found in the mouth.

Tongue prints, like fingerprints, are unique.

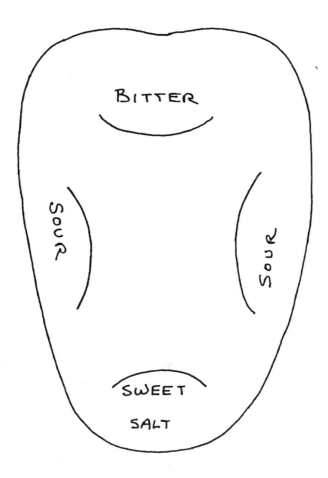

The Inside Story: A Look at Guts and Stuff

The Inside Story: A Look at Guts and Stuff

INFORMATION PLEASE

What goes on inside the body?

Inside the CHEST and ABDOMEN areas are the main functioning SYSTEMS of the body. These systems are made up of the main ORGANS along with their peripheral organs. The DIGESTIVE system provides nutrition to the body by breaking down food and making it ready for use by body cells. The CIRCULATORY system is responsible for moving food from the digestive system, and gases to and from the respiratory system. The RESPIRATORY system obtains oxygen from the atmosphere and returns carbon dioxide to the air. The NERVOUS system controls the working of all systems. The SKELETAL-MUSCULAR system holds up the body and allows us to do work and move. The ENDOCRINE system provides hormones that, along with the nervous system, control the working of all systems. The EXCRETORY system eliminates the wastes of metabolism through the kidneys. The REPRODUCTIVE system is the system that is responsible for sexual characteristics and for reproduction.

How does the digestive system work?

Digestion begins when food enters the mouth. Then the food moves down the ALIMENTARY CANAL to remove all nutrients. The first stop in the alimentary canal is the STOMACH. Here food is mixed with GASTRIC JUICES and HYDROCHLORIC ACID. These liquids kill bacteria and begin to digest the food. The food then passes into the SMALL INTESTINE where all the nutritional value is removed. The small intestine is a coiled tube that in an adult is about seven meters (23 feet) long. ENZYMES are released here by the LIVER, PANCREAS, and the intestine itself. These enzymes act further on food to reduce it to a form that can be passed through the wall of the intestine where it can be taken by the blood to the cells of the body. The residual material from the small intestine is pushed into the LARGE INTESTINE or COLON. The APPENDIX is found right at the beginning of this organ. Undigestible wastes enter the 1.5-meter (five-foot) colon where water is removed to be reused in the body. More solid wastes move to the end of the colon and are discharged through the RECTAL SPHINCTER. The colon is larger in diameter than the small intestine and materials move more slowly through it.

What causes problems in the digestive system?

A common problem of the digestive system is DIARRHEA, which results when food moves too quickly through the colon. INDIGESTION refers to nausea or bloating in the abdomen that is caused in part by eating the wrong foods, too much food, or not having eaten at all. CONSTIPATION results from too much water being taken from the material in the colon. This can be caused by a diet deficient in fiber or not enough liquid intake. FOOD POISONING is caused by a bacterium in poorly cooked or handled foods, often meats. Serious digestive problems require the help of a doctor. The PEDIATRICIAN is the most frequently used doctor for children's stomach problems. A GASTROENTEROLOGIST will handle the severe situations.

How does the respiratory system work?

The respiratory system is the mechanism by which gases are exchanged through the lungs to the blood or to the outside air. Air comes into the body through the NOSE or MOUTH, passes down the THROAT (PHARYNX), by the LARYNX or VOICE BOX through the TRACHEA, into the LUNGS. The passage keeps getting smaller, entering first into the BRONCHI, then the BRONCHIOLE, and finally into the tiny sacks called ALVEOLI. The lungs are filled with tiny air sacks and tiny blood vessels, so gases are exchanged at that point. The body wants the oxygen from the outside air and needs to rid itself of carbon dioxide produced through metabolism inside the cells. The carbon dioxide goes out the same way the oxygen came in. Water is also picked up in the lungs by the warm air; we always EXHALE water vapor (about .5 liters or one pint a day) along with the carbon dioxide.

What are some things that affect respiration?

Pollution affects respiration. Pollution, along with allergies, can have an impact on the breathing of young children. Respiratory problems among children generally occur in the winter when the crowded conditions of classrooms allow easy transmission of colds, sore throats, and flu. More serious problems occur when the simple childhood ailments develop further into BRONCHITIS or PNEUMONIA. SINUSITIS occurs when one of the sinus cavities in the head becomes further infected. A serious respiratory problem not related to infection is ASPHYXIATION, which is caused by the blockage of the airway either externally or internally. Everyone should learn the HEIMLICH MANEUVER that allows obstructions to be removed.

Want to know more about respiration?

Moist air helps breathing, as does fresh air. Adult lungs weigh about one kilogram (2 pounds). Healthy lungs are bright pink and spongy to the touch. A smoker's lungs will be black in spots. The lungs contain enough alveoli to cover a tennis court. The rib cage is the bone structure that protects both the heart and the lungs. An ordinary breath is .5 liters, while a deep breath is up to four liters. Ordinary, quiet breathing occurs about one breath for every four heartbeats or about 18-24 breaths per minute. Modifications of breathing are sighing, coughing, snoring, laughing, crying, hiccupping, and yawning. Can you add more? Professionals who work with respiratory problems are RESPIRATORY THERAPISTS, ALLERGISTS, and PULMONARY DISEASES DOCTORS.

To Catch a Breath

The lungs are the body's center for the exchange of gases. Oxygen in the air enters the circulatory system through the lungs. Waste—carbon dioxide—is carried by the blood to the lungs where it is exhaled. Another function of the lungs is to remove water from the body with each breath. You cannot see the water vapor as it is removed unless a cold surface is available. Breathe on a cold glass window in the winter and see what happens. Astronauts must remove the water vapor from breathing from their space craft. Campers will awaken on a cold morning with water droplets on the inside of the tent. All that moisture is coming from your breath and your lungs.

What to do

1. Ask the children to breathe in and out strongly.
2. What do you see? You should see nothing.
3. Can the children think of a time when they can see their breath? How about on a cold day?
4. What makes the breath visible? What do the children think it is? It is water vapor. Our lungs displace water from the body into the air.
5. On a cold, cold day the children can catch a large number of breaths on the window glass. Have the children take turns breathing on the window. Watch the water vapor collect and freeze. The colder the day, the better this will work.

Want to do more?

Create a similar situation with hot water. See the steam come off a teapot or cup of tea. On a winter day, take a walk and hunt for water vapor. Do this activity on different days with different temperatures. Talk about evaporation as the frost patch disappears.

> *Misty moisty,*
> *Fristy frosty,*
> *Breaths in winter weather.*
> *On the window,*
> *In the air,*
> *Breaths in winter weather.*

Language you can use

breath
exhale
water vapor
respiration

Things you will need

cold panes of glass on winter windows

How Big Is Your Chest?

Language you can use

measure
inhale
exhale
breathe
in
out
difference
predict
large
small
big
little

Things you will need

string or yarn
scissors
masking tape

What happens to your chest when you breathe in and breathe out? This activity goes beyond observation. It includes measurement, prediction, and comparison. With experience, the children will become increasingly accurate.

What to do

1. When we breathe air in through our mouth and nose, it travels into our lungs and expands our chest. We call this inhaling. When we breathe air out, it leaves our lungs and exits from our bodies through the mouth and nose. We call this exhaling.
2. How big do you think your chest can get when you inhale? Measure a child's relaxed chest measurement with a piece of string. How much longer will the string be when the child takes a DEEP breath? Cut a second piece of string to the length the children think it will be.
3. Place the child's name on a piece of masking tape. Use the tape to hang the first measurement and the string "estimate" on the wall where children can see it.
4. Now do an actual string measure of the expanded chest. Cut with scissors and place it next to the prediction. How do they compare?
5. Continue the activity with several more children. Does the accuracy of the predictions improve? Measure an adult. Is the prediction as accurate?

Want to do more?

You may want to use one color of string for actual measurements and another color for the predictions. Let children measure their parents' chest expansion. Bring the measurements to school and place them next to their own measurements.

Breathing Fast, Breathing Slow

Breathing has an important relationship to activity level. The more vigorous an activity is, the more air is needed. The ingredient in the air we use is oxygen, but breathing has another function. It removes carbon dioxide from the system. Carbon dioxide is one of the by-products of work. The more effort exerted, the more oxygen needed, and the more carbon dioxide created. Although an understanding of the exchange of gases is beyond the comprehension of young children, they can certainly explore breathing rates.

What to do

1. Ask the children whether they think that they will have to take more breaths after sitting or after running? Will their breathing be fast or slow when running? Fast or slow when sitting? Write down the children's predictions.
2. Let's do some things to find out if we're right. Have the children all breathe together. Count the number of breaths in ten seconds and record the number.
3. Now run in place as fast as possible. Together count the breaths. Record the results. Which has more? Are you breathing slowly or fast this time? Do you breathe faster when you sit or run? Which requires more air—running or sitting?

Want to do more?

Make a chart for each child—one column for at rest, another for after running. Count heartbeats or pulse rate after running and at rest. Can you make yourself breathe slowly after running?

Tisha, Tisha, run so fast.
How can she do it, just like that?
She breathes so hard in and out,
And runs right back with a shout.

Language you can use

fast
slow
breath
inhale
exhale
lungs
breathing

Things you will need

timer

paper and pen to record predictions

What Is Your Lung Capacity?

How much air do you think is contained in your lungs? The lungs are the body's organs that bring oxygen from the air into the body. Each time you breathe in, your rib cage expands to take air into the lungs. As you breathe out, the contents of the lungs are expelled. Lung capacity depends on body size, lung tissues, the diaphragm, and the health of your respiratory system.

Language you can use

lungs
capacity
observe
predict
measure
demonstrate
oxygen
air spirometer

Things you will need

two 2-liter plastic soda bottles with caps

2 1/2 feet (75 cm) of plastic tubing

plastic dishpan
water
35 mm film canister

What to do

1. Prepare the two-liter soda bottles. Cut the bottom off one bottle to form a funnel. Use the lids and the film canister to make a connector (see illustration).
2. Fill the two-liter bottle with water.
3. Fill the plastic dishpan with about five inches of water or enough to cover the water connector.
4. Cut a slit in the half bottle funnel for the plastic hose. Place one end of the hose in the funnel. Place the funnel into the water in the plastic tub. Use enough hose to go about 10 centimeters (4") into the funnel.
5. Hold your hand over the opening of the two-liter bottle. Turn the bottle upside down, keeping your hand over the opening so that no water can escape.
6. Place the bottle into the water in the dishpan and connect it to the funnel (see illustration).
7. Let the children predict the teacher's lung capacity. How much water will be forced out as he or she exhales?
8. The teacher takes a deep breath and exhales into the tube.
9. Children observe how accurate their predictions were by noting the water level in the two-liter inverted bottle. How much water was forced out?

Want to do more?

Are there other ways to measure what our lungs do? How about how far you can make a pencil roll with one blow?

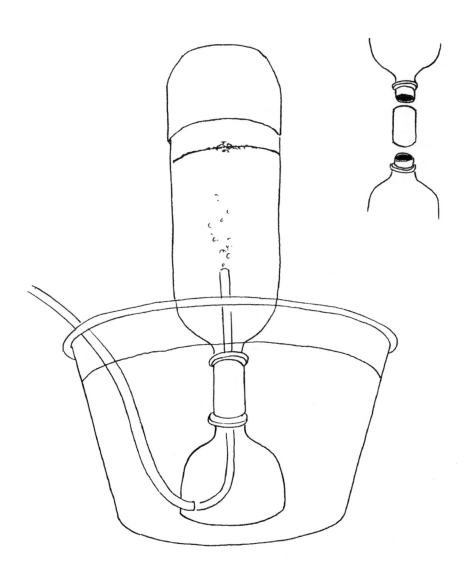

Hear a Heartbeat

Language you can use

stethoscope
heart
beat
sound
listen

Things you will need

pictures of the heart

drawing of a heart in a child's body

paper or plastic cups with the ends cut out so the ear will fit into the hole

a stethoscope or a picture of one
alcohol

When we think about hearing the heartbeat of a person, we usually think about a stethoscope. That is the instrument that doctors or nurses use when giving a medical examination. The doctor or nurse is listening to the heartbeat to determine if the sound of the heart is normal. Yes, healthy hearts make a certain, very easily identified sound as the valves of the heart open and close when the heart contracts and expands to force the blood out into the body. The sound the heart makes is a "lub dub, lub dub" sound. A stethoscope is a nice instrument to have because it allows the children to use a real scientific tool, but it is not necessary. A plain paper cup can do the same thing, though not quite as well. The cup forms an addition to the ear, just like the stethoscope, to channel sounds and transfer them up into the ear.

What to do

1. Ask the children if they know what the heart is and what it does. Bring out pictures of the heart and the heart represented in a drawing of a child's body. The heart is a muscle that is used to pump blood out to parts of the body. Ask how many of the children have had the doctor or nurse listen to their heart with a stethoscope. Show the stethoscope or a picture of the instrument. Discuss the fact that doctors use it to listen to the sounds of the heart and lungs.
2. Now they are going to have a chance to listen to the heart of a friend. We do not have a stethoscope for everyone, so a cup will be used to pick up the sounds of the heart.
3. Divide the children into pairs. Have them point to the position on one another's chest of each other where the heart can be found. When they can all point out the heart's location, give each pair a cup stethoscope. Show them how to listen, and have each child take a turn to listen for his or her partner's heartbeat.
4. Some problem solving that must be done to hear well is to reduce sounds made by hitting the cup with fingers, cloth, and accidental movements. The children will find that these sounds are also amplified by the cup.
5. Go around to each pair to determine if they are in the right area to hear the heart and if they, in fact, are hearing the heartbeat. If you have a stethoscope, let each child use it after finding the heartbeat with the cup stethoscope. Be sure to clean the ear pieces with alcohol for each child.

Want to do more?

Count the heartbeats per minute. An infant will have up to 140 beats per minute while an adult will have around 72 beats per minute. Can you distinguish the "lub dub" sound? Talk about pulse and its relationship to heartbeat.

Heartbeat Listeners— The Advanced Model

The stethoscope is a device doctors use to listen to our hearts and lungs when we go for a health checkup. This activity shows how to make a simple yet functional stethoscope to enhance hearing the sound of the heart as compared to using the ear alone.

What to do

1. Talk about health checkup visits. What happens? Encourage the children to share their experiences. Frequently, doctors use stethoscopes for listening to the heartbeat.
2. Ask the children to try to find a friend's heartbeat just by using their ear. It won't be easy.
3. Now let's try to find the heartbeat with a stethoscope.
4. Distribute plastic squeeze bottles that have had the bottom half of the bottle removed. Distribute rubber tubing. Instruct the children to attach one end of the tubing to the spout top of the squeeze bottle. Now the stethoscope is ready to use.
5. Place the wide end of the bottle (funnel) on the chest. Place the open end of the rubber tubing in one ear. The children should move the stethoscope about the chest until they find the location where the heartbeat is strongest. This is the center of the chest between the lungs, just under the breast bone.
6. Remember, it may be difficult for the children to find the heartbeat. If they can't locate it, let them jump in place several times and then try again.

NOTE: Be sure to wipe off the end of the tube with alcohol before it touches another child's ear.

Language you can use

listen
stethoscope
heart
heartbeat
sound
doctor
ear
chest

Things you will need

funnels or plastic mustard squeeze bottles with the bottoms cut out

soft rubber or plastic tubing (available at hardware stores)

scissors
tape
alcohol

Want to do more?

Let the children hear an adult heartbeat and compare it to their own. Which beats faster, slower? What else can they hear with their stethoscopes? Go on a sound discovery tour of the room.

The average adult heart weighs about 12 ounces.

Over, Under, Beside, On Top— Where Is Your Heart?

Language you can use

over
under
beside
next to
behind
in front of
above
below

Things you will need

Valentine hearts with the children's names on them—the real heart is about the size of a fist, so make them about that size

a picture of a real heart

Relative position in space is an important concept to scientists. In fact, it is a major key to communication for all of us. By using paper hearts and a happy day for children, Valentine's Day, we can enjoy this activity with all our hearts.

What to do

1. Ask the children to tell you what they know about the heart. Do they know where it is? The sound it makes?
2. Show them the picture of the heart. Tell them that the heart is an organ in the body about the size of your fist. The function of the heart is to pump blood through the body. The location of the heart is the chest. What are the differences between human hearts and Valentine hearts?
3. Give a paper heart to each of the children to play a "Simon Says" follow-the-leader game that can go like this:

- Put your heart over your head.
- Put your heart under your arm.
- Put your heart beside your leg.
- Put your heart behind your back.
- Put your heart in front of your eyes.
- Put your heart below your waist.
- Put your heart above your shoulder.
- Put your heart next to your real heart.

Want to do more?

Use other body organs. Have an organ of the month. Pair or group children to do the activity during free time. Speed up or slow down the activity.

The heart pumps about five quarts of blood per minute. This can rise to 20 quarts a minute during strenuous exercise. Your heart beats more than 36 million times a year.

A Naval Experience: Belly Button Prints

The belly button or navel is the point at which the umbilical cord was attached from the mother to the child. Through this cord, all nutrients, gases, and excretory materials passed as the child was carried in the womb. When the child was born, this cord was cut. The remnant fell away from the child, leaving the belly button as a scar. Each of us has one and everyone will have one when they are born. Some are indented, others pushed out. Which one do you have? Shall we classify our belly buttons?

NOTE: This activity might be best in warm weather when children are wearing less clothing. Some children may be hesitant to pull up their shirts for this activity. If so, respect their wishes.

What to do

1. Ask the children what they know about the belly button or navel. What is it for? Do we all have belly buttons?
2. Explain how the belly button came to be. The belly button was part of what connected us to our mothers before we were born.
3. Our belly buttons are like our fingerprints. They are different for every person. Let's make prints of belly buttons.
4. Give each child a small ball of soft playdough. Have one of the children place the dough on a table and bend over it, placing her navel in the center. Push down, spreading out the dough and making a print. Put the name on the print and set out to dry.
5. Go through the entire class, making everyone's navel print.

Want to do more?

Sort the prints, remembering that prints are the reverse of the "real" thing. Can you classify these prints? How about "Ins" and "Outs"? Are all navels different?

What's the only button that you can never lose? Your belly button.

Language you can use

umbilical
belly button
print
navel

Things you will need

soft playdough

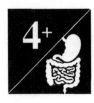

Organ Finders

Language you can use

organs
heart
liver
lungs
stomach
intestines

Things you will need

plastic term paper covers
hole punch
yarn
permanent markers

The body has many organs that help to keep us alive and healthy. These organs have names that some children will be familiar with while others may be hearing them for the first time. In this activity, we will name and locate organs that the children can relate to and give brief simple explanations as to their functions.

What to do

1. Teacher prepares organ transparency "aprons" made from term paper covers by drawing the organs on them with a permanent marker (see illustration).
2. Let the children help punch holes in the plastic and thread the yarn ties.
3. Assist the children in hanging the aprons over their necks and tying the straps. The organs drawn on the apron should approximate the size of the child's actual organs.
4. Then the teacher could say, "If we could see inside our bodies, under our skin and bones, we would find our organs. I've marked the location of your organs on the organ transparency. I'll touch them and name them. This is your heart." The teacher touches the heart on the transparency. Now put your hand on your heart. Can you feel it beating? Your heart is a muscle that pumps blood all through your body.
5. "This is your stomach." The teacher touches the stomach location on the organ transparency. Now you touch your stomach. The stomach is where our food is digested. Follow this same procedure for other organs.

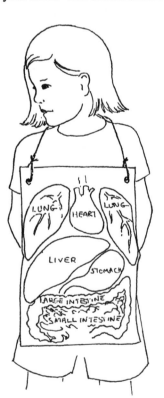

- *Lungs:* Our lungs breathe air in and out of our bodies.
- *Liver:* Our liver helps with digestion and helps to keep our blood clean.
- *Intestines:* Help to digest our food.

Want to do more?

See if the children can find approximate organ locations without the use of the plastic organ transparency. Add other organs, for example, kidneys, appendix.

Dogs Aren't the Only Ones That Growl

All the food we eat passes though the stomach and on to the intestines. The digestive system makes noises as it does its job. The noise is caused by acids and gas as food is passed though the intestines. Muscular contractions called PERISTALSIS also make noises. The food is broken down into nutrients that will be filtered into the blood stream, and waste that will be excreted when we go to the toilet.

What to do

1. Discuss how food passes from our mouths into the esophagus, stomach, and intestines. As acids and gases interact with food to break it down, noises are made. Sometimes people will say, "My stomach is growling."
2. Give each child a cup with the bottom removed. Group the children in pairs. Let's use our cup listeners to find out if we can hear some growling. Remember dogs aren't the only ones that growl.
3. Demonstrate how to use the cup as a listening device. The cup will enhance the sound quality as it funnels into the cup and passes directly to the listening ear.
4. Now put your cup to your ear and move it around on your partner's abdomen. Listen carefully. What do you hear?
5. As the children listen, ask them to describe the sounds they hear. Ask them to try to imitate the sounds.
6. Compare sound descriptions.

Want to do more?

Listen to other sounds that the body makes. Listen to the heart, legs, neck, back.

When you get hungry, your stomach muscles begin to contract. If there is air in your stomach, it may make a rumbling noise as it churns.

Language you can use

stomach
intestines
sound
listen
listeners
hear
digestion
pass
through
acid
gas
peristalsis

Things you will need

paper cups with bottoms removed

A Noisy Body Working

Language you can use

sound
stethoscope
works
swallow
chew
stomach
growl
heartbeat

Things you will need

toilet paper rolls
carrots or another crunchy
food

The growing child's body is not a silent one. Just an awareness of those sounds, as evidence that the body is working, is a way to allow children to obtain knowledge that will make sense of the doctor's probes and pushes at later visits. The body makes all sorts of natural sounds that mean something to the trained person.

What to do

1. Show the children how to use the toilet paper roll as a stethoscope to hear sounds made by our bodies.
2. Ask the children to identify times that they hear the body working, for example, when chewing.
3. Choose some children to chew, and have other children place their stethoscope tubes on a chewing child's cheek to listen to the sounds. Talk about these sounds. They are the sounds of teeth working.
4. What other sounds of the body working can you and the children think of? Some might be swallowing, stomach growling, bones/joints creaking, heart beating, lips smacking, and breathing. Explore as many of these as you can.

Want to do more?

Bring in a real stethoscope. Record sounds of the body. List some body workings that make no sounds. Could there be sounds you might not be able to hear?

Head to Toe: Everything Goes Together

Head to Toe: Everything Goes Together

INFORMATION PLEASE

The WHOLE BODY is a very important concept because nothing in the human body works alone. This book has a chapter on each of the sensory areas of the body, but the nose cannot function without the mouth, the brain, the heart, or the stomach. In the body, nothing really works alone, but that is a difficult concept for the young child to understand.

What are the systems of the body?

Scientists and physicians have created divisions of the body in order to more easily study the body and understand its functions. These divisions of the body, called SYSTEMS, are NERVOUS, RESPIRATORY, DIGESTIVE, CIRCULATORY, EXCRETORY, REPRODUCTIVE, HEPATIC, ENDOCRINE, and SKELETAL /MUSCULAR.

How does your body communicate with itself?

The center of the NERVOUS system is the BRAIN, which was first described by Hippocrates over 2500 years ago. Scientists believe that all human behavior happens through a series of electrochemical impulses within this system. Nerve cells, NEURONS, are the building blocks of this system. Many neurons are banded together like a cable to form a NERVE. The microscopic gap area at the end of a nerve cell where it joins another is called a SYNAPSE. Tiny sacs on the neurons are stimulated to produce chemical messengers that allow impulses to travel to the next neurons. The main division (CENTRAL NERVOUS SYSTEM) is located in the skull (BRAIN) and spine (SPINAL CORD), while the PERIPHERAL NERVOUS SYSTEM is the nerve network that fills the rest of the body, sending and receiving impulses from outside sources or from the other body systems. Body actions known as REFLEXES as well as the AUTONOMIC NERVOUS system are controlled by the peripheral system.

The BRAIN and NERVOUS SYSTEM send impulses to and from the eye through the OPTIC NERVE, the nose through the OLFACTORY NERVE, the ear through the AUDITORY NERVE, the taste buds in the mouth through the GUSTATORY NERVE, and the nerve receptors in the skin through the PERIPHERAL NERVES in the skin. Through this network of nerves, spinal cord, and brain we all receive, store, and react to the STIMULI from the environment. When enough experiences have occurred and in the right sequences, we store the memories in the brain to be recalled when needed.

How do the respiratory and circulatory systems interact?

The RESPIRATORY and CIRCULATORY systems work together to exchange carbon dioxide and oxygen in all parts of the body. The circulatory system is also the major pathway for food and waste to be taken to and from the cells of the body. The RESPIRATORY, or gas exchange system, is centered around the LUNGS and the hollow tube leading to the lungs from the nose and mouth. The TRACHEA branches at the opening to the two lungs into BRONCHIAL TUBES that lead to smaller tubes, BRONCHIOLI, finally ending in the tiny sacks (ALVEOLI) where the air is exchanged with the blood.

The circulatory system consists of the HEART, a complex muscular pump, the blood vessels that carry blood to and from the heart, and the BLOOD. The heart has four chambers that function together to pump blood out away from the heart through ARTERIES and back through VEINS. Like the respiratory tubes, the arteries and veins become smaller as they move away from the heart, finally ending in the CAPILLARIES where the real work of the circulatory system begins. The capillaries and ALVEOLI meet in the lungs to exchange gases. Capillaries surround the small intestine and absorb food as it passes through the walls of the digestive tract; capillaries also exchange wanted and unwanted materials and chemical regulators throughout the body.

What about those other systems?

Other systems that interact with the circulatory system are the endocrine, hepatic, and excretory that help to clean the body and maintain bodily functions. One cannot function without the other, as the ENDOCRINE system adds special chemicals called HORMONES that affect growth, control and monitor chemical balance, and help the body make proper responses to changes from the outside world. The ENDOCRINE GLANDS are the PITUITARY, ADRENAL, THYROID, THYMUS, PARATHYROID, PANCREAS, and OVARIES or TESTES.

The EXCRETORY system, whose primary organ is the KIDNEY, removes wastes from the BLOOD, voiding through the BLADDER and the URINARY TRACT. The HEPATIC system is sometimes considered as a part of the digestive system. Its main organ, the LIVER, is the largest gland in the body. It functions to store and regulate sugar, change fat and amino acids, filter and clean the blood, and produce bile.

The digestive system has been described in the internal organs section, and, as you can see, is heavily dependent on the other systems. The SKELETAL/MUSCULAR system is the structural support for the body; without it we could not move about. BONES also form the protective skeleton surrounding and protecting the fragile parts of the body.

Finally, the REPRODUCTIVE system allows humans to reproduce. Each sex has a different reproductive organ. The male's are called the TESTES and are located in the SCROTUM. The female organs are the OVARIES and are located in the lower abdomen. Both organs are found in the same area as the EXCRETORY system.

While the importance of the auto-immune system is not within the grasp of very young children, the impact of AIDS-related illnesses surely has been and will continue to be a concern of health and body learning for many years to come. The IMMUNE system is the part of the body that gives us the ability to fend off sickness or disease. Awareness of the immune system can be extended to children by attention to cleanliness, safety, and shot records.

But nothing in the WHOLE BODY works by itself. Each of us is a whole organism with a complex and interactive body of incredible complexity. Children may not be able to understand that complexity, but they surely can appreciate the uniqueness of the whole body.

Monkey Listen, Monkey Do, and in a Mirror Too

Language you can use

follow
point
body part names

Things you will need

large mirror
tape recording
made by the
teacher asking
the children to
point at or move
parts of the body

The youngest children in your room can look at themselves in the mirror and learn about their bodies. This activity uses the mirror as the tool of observation, and it teaches the body parts through the mirror and, thus, the child's own body.

What to do

1. Bring two to three children to the largest mirror in the room. From the group, choose a child who knows the body parts fairly well. This leader can model for the other children.
2. Have the children listen to the tape and do what the tape says. The children are to follow the directions in unison; they can watch each other. The tape can start from the head, the eyes, ears, mouth, and chin and move down the body. When reaching the toes, begin to name parts all over the body. Repeat all body parts twice, with the lesser known ones more frequently.

Want to do more?

Have the children give instructions. Add things like right and left to the tape. Add movement. Help the children make their own tape. Explore the reversal that occurs in mirrors.

Owies

Cuts and scratches are common occurrences with young children. This activity takes a close-up view of these injuries. In the process of observing and comparing, the children learn that as time passes the body heals.

What to do

1. When a child has been injured, let him or her share with the rest of the class how the wound was inflicted.
2. Discuss what we do to help wounds heal and how to avoid infection. Talk about the importance of washing a wound and keeping it clean.
3. Mark days off on the "Get Better Calendar" until the wound is completely healed.
4. Emphasize that the healing process is enhanced by good first aid and hygiene.

Want to do more?

Share scars—discuss how they were obtained. Has anyone had stitches? Trees develop scars where they've lost a branch or been injured. Can you find some tree scars?

Language you can use

cuts
scratches
wounds
blood
bleed
observe
heal
clear
wash
bandage
band aid
antiseptic
scab
skin

Things you will need

magnifying glass
a "Get Better Calendar"

Nit Picking

Language you can use

lice
nit
infestation
pediculosis
louse
itch

Things you will need

pictures of insects and animals
pictures of head lice available from the companies listed on the next page.

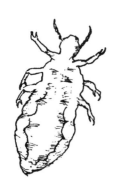

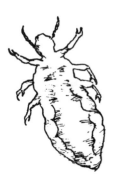

The second most common communicable disease of public schools is head lice infestation. Six to twelve million cases of head lice will occur in U.S. schools each year. Most of these cases occur from August to November, but they can happen all year round. One half of the children with infestation have family members who have lice. Lice present a problem, but they also present a teachable moment. Don't you just itch to get started? Teaching, that is, or maybe you already ITCH.

What to do

1. Don't wait for a lice infestation to occur in the school. You don't want to highlight a particular child's or children's problem.

2. Begin your discussion of head lice by asking the children what they know about animals. Make a list on the board of the characteristics of animals.
- Animals move.
- Animals get food.

List kinds of animals and characteristics of these animals. Since the louse is an insect, have the children name and share information about insects. because a louse is an insect. Focus the discussion and sharing on what they know about the insect animal group.

3. What do we know about insects? Can we name some insects? You will want to have pictures of common insects. Point out the characteristics of insects:
- Three body regions—head, thorax, abdomen
- Six pairs of legs
- Some way to eat (mouth)
- Usually antennae
- Many have wings

Insects: fly, butterfly, mosquito, beetle, grasshopper, lightning bug. Try to have pictures of these bugs.

5. Let's look at the insect that might cause our school a problem. Put up a picture of a louse.

6. This is what causes heads to itch, and why we sometimes check everyone's heads to see if lice are there. But these insects, lice, are so small that we can hardly see them. What the teacher or nurse is looking for when she checks hair are not the lice but the eggs of the lice. We can see them, they are white and attached to the hair. They are called "Nits."

7. Look at the picture of the lice, count the legs, find the three body parts, the mouth, very faint eyes. Lice do not like light. Look at the legs. Lice have legs that are especially built to hold onto and move about the hair on your head. Explain that shelter for the lice, their house, is our hair. Lice especially like to live in the hair at the nape of the neck, behind the ears, and the crown of the head. They eat liquid from the bites they make on your skin. Lice have

many children, so they always look for new homes, that is, new heads. This is why we don't share combs and brushes.

Want to do more?

Investigate other insects. What are ways to keep ourselves healthy?

Want to know more?

Some things children and parents need to know about lice are that they:
1. Can live off the human body only 48 hours.
2. Live at 98.6 degrees F or 22 degrees C; they die at lower and higher temperatures.
3. Don't like moisture or high humidity.
4. Cannot be found on other animals.
5. Cannot jump.
6. Can infest anyone, but children with long hair are most easily infested.

School Policy Recommendations:

1. Have a written policy on lice infestation.
2. Have a "No NIT" policy.
3. Develop an education policy for children and parents.
4. Have a comb and brush for each child.
5. Have separate hangers or coat hooks as well as individual cots and blankets.
6. Don't forget to treat dress-up clothes during an outbreak.

Companies to contact

Copley Pharmaceutical Inc.
Consumer Products Division
25 John Road
Canton, MA 02021

Guidelines for Treating Lice
    Infestations
c/o Christine Bridges
Reed and Carnrick
One New England Avenue
Piscataway, NJ 08855

Nix Leaflet Offer
c/o Ogilvy and Mather
450 Park Avenue South
New York, NY 10016

RID Educational Services
c/o Sweeney and Partners
One Paragon Drive
Montvale, NJ 07645

Smith Kline Beecham
Prof. Services Department
P.O. Box 1467
Pittsburgh, PA 15230-9912

Puppet Power

Language you can use

body part names (arm, leg, etc.)

Things you will need

body design page (see illustration)

fasteners
many colors of construction paper

butter tubs to hold cut body pieces

large drawing of the completed body (labeled)

crayons

Motion and movement of the body are replicable through puppets. This activity allows the children to complete a body parts puppet, to match the names of the body parts, and to see how the human body movements can be shown though moving a puppet. Fun and language follow the puppet's movements, making this activity a real winner.

What to do

1. Have parents or grandparents cut out the body pieces from construction paper. Place the parts in separate containers. Label the containers. Place an enlarged drawing of the completed body on the wall.
2. Help the children assemble the body parts into a puppet. They will need two arms, two legs, two hands, two feet, and one body. Make the puppet any color.
3. As they select each part, talk about the names of the parts.
4. Remember that each arm and leg will have two parts. The children can look at the large-sized sample to see if they have a complete body.
5. When the assembly is completed, they can add facial and other body characteristics.

Want to do more?

Do storytelling with the puppets. Place the body in running positions, throwing position, sitting position. Analyze a running movement; use four to five puppets to replicate this motion.

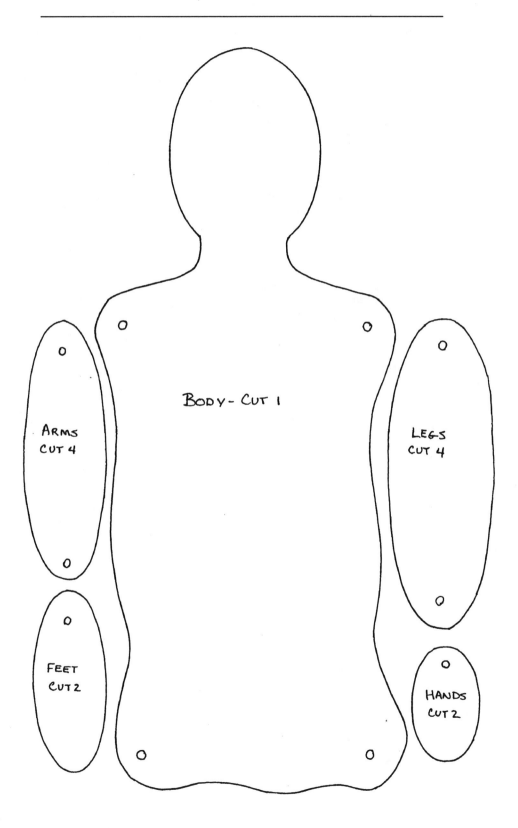

BODY- CUT 1

ARMS
CUT 4

LEGS
CUT 4

FEET
CUT 2

HANDS
CUT 2

Tracing Body Spaces

Language you can use

body
larger
smaller
space
size

Things you will need

colored chalk
large blacktop or
concrete area

This activity puts a new twist on body tracing by asking the children to experiment with body space as a variable. They make their bodies as large as they can, then as small as they can. How can two such different outlines be of the same person?

What to do

1. Ask the children to make themselves the biggest they can be. They will do this by standing on tiptoes, sucking in air, and so on. Then ask them to make themselves small. What do they do?
2. How do you tell if you are bigger or smaller? If we want to be scientific, then we must be more exact. One way to record shapes is to lie on the ground and trace around the body with chalk.
3. How do you think you can make the biggest shape? The smallest shape? Have each predict this shape.
4. Now we shall see. One by one have the children lie down in their smallest shape. Trace around them in one color. Then have them assume the biggest, largest shape. Trace again with a different color.
5. Look at the two separate shapes. Which was the largest? Was the prediction accurate?

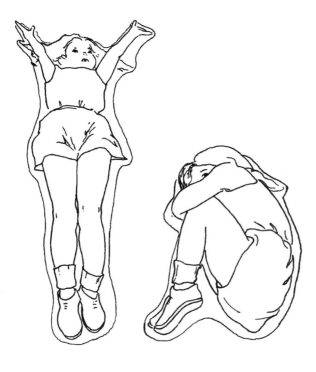

Want to do more?

After watching others, can they make a smaller space? A larger one? Who makes the largest size, smallest? Which part of the body makes the biggest or smallest space? Trace it.

Measure Me Growth Chart

The development of a positive self-concept is an integral part of any curriculum. This activity is not to be used in a competitive way among children. It's to be used to show the child his or her own personal gains in growth over a specified time period.

What to do

1. Tape a strip of adding machine tape vertically on the wall. As one child stands next to the wall, another child or the teacher makes a mark on the chart, indicating the child's height. Note the date. Make a separate strip for each child.
2. Repeat this activity every two or three months, using the same tape each time. Growth over time will become apparent.
3. Compare the amounts the children have grown.

Want to do more?

Make a weight chart or a hair length chart.

Most girls stop growing when they are about 18. Most boys continue growing for a few more years.

Language you can use

measure
tall
long
short
high
inches
feet
time
days
months
years
centimeters
meters

Things you will need

tape
measuring ruler
pencil

adding machine tape

Denoting Family Demographics:
A Graphing Experience

Language you can use

family
size
large
number
how many

Things you will need

large graph paper

squares cut from construction paper to fit graph paper squares

glue or paste

Each child has a family. These families vary in size and may grow or get smaller as the school year progresses. This activity lets children collect and share information about family size, and enables the entire class to graph the collective results. Remember, families come in all different sizes, and it doesn't matter how big or little your family is. A child's perception may include extended families and nonrelatives.

What to do

1. Discuss and share information about family size. Some are larger, some are smaller. Families may include step-parents, grandparents, siblings, and other relatives and nonrelatives. Some family members may live with the children, others may not. Talk about similarities and differences in a supportive and positive way.
2. Give each child colored construction paper squares.
3. Let them place one square on a bar graph for each member of their family. The resulting colorful bar graph will reveal the family sizes of the children.

Want to do more?

Use different colored squares for sisters, brothers, uncles, etc. How many uncles are in your family? Make a bar graph on pets in the family.

Body Book

Creating a "Body Book" supports children's emerging literacy skills while focusing on the body. It reinforces the similarities and differences of the various body parts. Let the children take their books home to share with their families.

What to do

1. Tell the children they are going to make a picture book. They will be the authors. The picture book will be about bodies. Discuss the various body parts.
2. Direct the children to find and cut out pictures of a specific body part. Select a different body part each day.
3. Glue pictures to a sheet of paper, using one page for eyes, one page for mouths, one page for hands, and so on. Let the children write or dictate captions for the pages. Conclude the book with a few pages of whole bodies.
4. Slip two picture pages into each resealable plastic bag. Staple the bags together through the seals (see illustration).
5. Let the children share their books with each other.

Want to do more?

Make a body mural, make animal body books, or make a body puzzle by cutting apart a body figure mounted on cardboard.

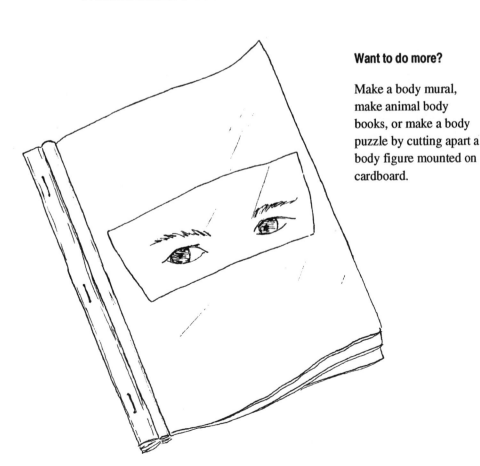

Language you can use

books
pictures
body parts
eyes
nose
ears
mouth
legs
feet
internal organs
hands

Things you will need

catalogs and magazines

scissors
glue

crayons and markers

standard writing paper

large resealable plastic bags to match the size of the paper

Balancing Bodies

Language you can use

balance
beam
predict
walked
down
up
towel

Things you will need

board 10 centimeters (4") wide and about 1 meter (3') long

a fulcrum—a large wooden block or piece of two by four or four by four

Children are involved in balancing activities over and over during play both at home and at school. They use balance as they climb, build with blocks, and carry things. This activity encourages scientific exploration as the children predict, infer, and observe bodies in quest of balance.

What to do

1. Place the board on the fulcrum with one end touching the ground.
2. Ask the children if they think they can keep both ends from touching the ground while standing on it.
3. Ask them to predict what they will need to do to make it balance—with one person, two persons, three persons, four persons.
4. The children now attempt to balance in the above sequence.
5. Encourage them to make inferences as they observe the action. Why do you think it's balanced? Why do you think it's not balanced?

Want to do more?

Let children use building blocks to make the board balance. Let them predict or make inferences just as they did before.

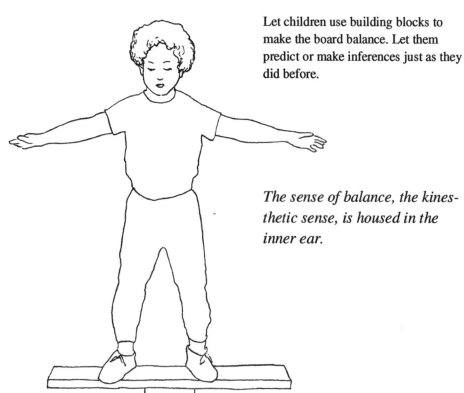

The sense of balance, the kinesthetic sense, is housed in the inner ear.

Body Sculpting

Body sculpting is a delightful way to teach children the body part names, and, more importantly, involve them in the process of communication. It provides the opportunity to practice giving and following directions. Once children understand the process, body sculpting is great for little snatches of time normally wasted.

What to do

1. Group the children into pairs. Use one child to demonstrate the activity.
2. Tell the children that they are going to make a sculpture using their friend's body. This is done by one of the partners moving the other's body parts into positions which are to be held. Here's a sample: "Take the left hand and place it on the right shoulder." Move the child so the hand is in the correct place. Ask the other children to follow. "Tip your partner's head over to touch the left hand." "Put one foot in front of the other."
3. Look! We have a room full of statues.
4. Let someone else be the leader.

Want to do more?

Have a child sculpt two or three children. Make a sculpture of people sitting or lying on the floor. Can the whole group make a giant statue?

Language you can use

body part names
directional words—up, down, in front of, etc.

Things you will need

A Bare Bones Comparison

Language you can use

bones
X-ray
skeleton
classify
sort
long
short
flat
irregular
different
fit
small
large
wide
chunky
curved

Things you will need

X-rays of body—whole body and individual sections

real skeleton if possible

chicken bones

There are more than two hundred bones in your body. Each is fitted for its own particular place and function. All bones can be classified into four basic groups.
- Long bones that are thin with swollen ends; these are also lightly curved so they can support more weight, for example, arms, legs, fingers.
- Short bones that are wide and chunky, for example, feet and wrists.
- Flat bones that are plate-like, for example, ribs and shoulder blades.
- Irregular bones that don't fit into any of the above three groups, for example, vertebrae, ear bones.

What to do

1. Examine the X-rays. Can the children find the places on their own bodies shown in the X-rays?
2. Compare human X-rays of bones to chicken bones. Talk about the similarities.
3. Sort the actual bones into the four classifications: long bones, short bones, flat bones, and irregular bones.
4. Discuss the functions of various bones. Think of your skeleton as a person without skin and muscles. What would your body be like with no bones? What would your skeleton be like with no body to hold it together?

Want to do more?

Can you think of animals without bones? Bring in other bones for the children to examine.

Want to know more?

At birth, we have 270 bones. By adulthood we have 206 bones because some of them fuse together. Half of our bones are in the hands and feet. Long bones allow us to run, walk, throw. These bones are strong, but also light for their size, because they are mostly hollow inside. If they were solid, the increased weight would slow us down considerably. These bones are thicker at the ends as these parts fit the ends of adjoining bones.

A Joint Adventure

The skeleton of the human body is comprised of a series of different kinds of bones hooked together by joints. These joints allow the body to be flexible and to give various parts specific jobs. Just how many joints do we have? Move your bodies and find out.

What to do

1. Talk about joints as places where our bones move. Can the children think of some joints in their own bodies? Show the tummy moving in and out or the tongue curling and compare that to a joint moving at the elbow or knee.
2. Mark the elbow joint on the drawing. Then the knee joint.
3. Wiggle your way through the entire body looking for joints. Make a mark on the drawing for each joint found. Have the children move the joints as they are identified.

Want to do more?

Sing the song "Them Bones," and move the joints as you sing. Identify different kinds of joints, such as ball and socket. Look at the joints in a chicken wing.

Language you can use

joint
move
elbow joint
knee joint
bone
skeleton
bend

Things you will need

an outline drawing of a child on butcher paper
crayons

Go on a Bone Hunt

Language you can use

bones
bodies
hunt
explore
mark

Things you will need

washable bold color markers
swimming suits or shorts
wading pool or sprinkler

Dogs like to hunt for bones that they can chew on for snacks. Children like to go on hunts, too. This activity offers a hands-on experience to let the children explore areas of their bodies in which they can see and feel bones. This activity is best done on a warm day. Following the activity, a jump in the pool or a run under the sprinkler will leave bodies sparkling clean.

What to do

1. On a warm day have the children put on their swimming suits.
2. Pass out one washable color marker to each child.
3. With your fingers, hunt on your body to find your bones.
4. When you feel a bone, make a line. Only make lines where you feel the bones.
5. The children point to the lines (bones) on their bodies. The teacher then names the bones that have been marked. Probable bones are kneecap or patella, ribs, sternum, collar bone, clavicles, scapulas, vertebra, backbone, humerus, elbow, radius, wrist, carpals, metacarpal, phalanges, and tarsal.
6. After the bone hunt, let the children jump into the wading pool or take a run under the sprinkler to wash off their bone markings.

Want to do more?

Put labels on a Halloween skeleton. For example, this bone is called the patella (kneecap)—touch child's knee—then place the label on the paper skeleton.

The leg bones (femurs) are the biggest bones in your body.

When you're grown your body will have 206 bones.

Body Beat

It's fun to listen to music and to keep the beat by tapping our toes or clapping our hands. Here's a way to enjoy music and rhythm while reinforcing the names of body parts.

What to do

1. Play music with a strong, steady beat. Practice clapping in time to the music.
2. The leader, an adult or child, points to a body part and gives directions such as "click your tongue," "tap your feet," or "pat your stomach."
3. The children keep the beat with the selected body part until the leader changes it with a new direction.
4. See how many new sounds your group can create.

Want to do more?

How many silent ways can you use your body to keep time with the music? Develop patterns such as "clap, stomp, clap, stomp."

Language you can use

music
keep
beat
rhythm
clap
stomp
feet
hands
lips
click
tongue
tap
fingers
smack
stomach

Things you will need

picture of body

records of songs that have a variety of tempos

Find a Hot Spot

Language you can use

temperature
thermometer
higher
lower
normal

Things you will need

thermometer
alcohol
cotton
chart of the body
crayons

How do children have their temperature taken? Yes, it is usually taken in the mouth with a thermometer because that location allows the most accurate temperature taking and is the most typical of real body temperature for the rest of the body. Are the temperatures the same on all other parts of the body? Shall we find out if the temperature of the finger tip is 37.5 degrees Celsius or 98.6 degrees Fahrenheit? Which part of the body is the coldest?

What to do

1. Show the children the typical thermometer. In order to use the metric system, try to find one using the Celsius scale. The metric thermometer has the advantage of lower numbers with a wider range.
2. Take a child's temperature with the thermometer. Read the temperature and show the child how this is done. Reading the thermometer is a skill that must be taught. Repeat until the skill is learned or record the value yourself if the children are unable to perform the task. Remember to wipe the thermometer with alcohol before the next child uses it.
3. Now look at temperatures of the body's extremities. Choose four to five locations where the temperature can be taken. You could choose under the arm, in the fist, between the toes, behind the ear, on the stomach, or in the arm. Find the temperature of each spot and plot those values on a body chart.
4. Try to develop a statement about the temperature of the human body from your observations. It should go something like this: the temperature drops as you move away from the core of the body.

Want to do more?

Try your pets. Do they show the same traits?

Mirror Feelings

Our feelings are shown in many ways—by our voices and by our total body language. This activity focuses on the face as a "feeling expresser."

What to do

1. Have the children look in the mirror while the teacher describes different events and situations.
2. Ask the children to express feelings by facial movements as they react to the events described. For example:

> It's time to go to bed!
> It's time to get up!
> You can stay up one hour past your bedtime tonight.
> Here's your birthday present.
> You've just been scolded.
> We're having (your least favorite food) for dinner.
> We're going out for lunch.
> You are going to stay with the baby sitter tonight.
> Grandma and Grandpa are coming over tonight.

3. Once the children understand the game, encourage them to suggest ideas.

Want to do more?

Discuss how our pets express their feelings of happiness, disappointment, and sadness.

It takes 17 muscles to smile, 43 muscles to frown, and more than 200 muscles to take one step.

> **Hearts, Like Doors**
> *Hearts, like doors, will open with ease*
> *To very, very little keys,*
> *And don't forget that two of these*
> *Are "Thank you, friend" and "If you*
> *   please."*

Language you can use

feelings
face
expression
listen
hear
mirror
reflection

Things you will need

hand-held mirror for each child

Food Coverups

Foods are important to help us grow and to keep our bodies healthy and strong. The way we feel about ourselves is also important. A healthy self-concept also contributes to our overall well-being. This activity is all about you and the food you eat. Cover your body with your favorite foods—they make you feel good all over. Some of your favorite foods will be different from the other children's favorites. That's okay. The foods you like are the foods YOU like.

Language you can use

food
cut
trace
body
like
dislike
paste
share
partner

Things you will need

butcher paper
crayons
paste
scissors

magazines with food pictures

food ads from newspapers

selected catalogs of fruits and vegetables

What to do

1. The children choose partners.
2. Each child traces around his partner on a sheet of white butcher paper. With younger children, an adult should do the tracing.
3. The children cut out pictures of food from magazines and paste the pictures to their own body tracing. Foods should be those that they enjoy eating.
4. Let the children share their favorite foods by showing their traced bodies and the foods they have chosen.
5. Talk about foods that have been selected. Some will be different than others. It's okay. We are all different in many ways. Our likes and dislikes of certain foods are just another difference that we have.
6. Discuss the basic four food groups. Let the children classify the foods they have on their cutout bodies into the four food groups.

Want to do more?

Do the same activity with snack foods, foods I like for breakfast, foods I like for lunch, and so on.

My Favorite Things

As we talk to others and share our feelings about many things, we often speak about those that are our favorites. It might be food, family, friends, animals, toys, weather, and anything else that we are particularly fond of. This activity lets each child choose pictures of his or her favorite things and then put them into a creative work of art that can be taken home to be shared with parents.

What to do

1. Discuss favorite things during circle or small group time.
2. Let children tear or cut with scissors pictures from magazines and catalogs. You may want to cut pictures for very young children.
3. Give each child a cardboard wheel. They arrange the pictures and glue or paste them where they choose.
4. Give the children the opportunity to dictate comments about their favorite things. Write these comments on a separate piece of paper and attach to the wheel.
5. Talk about which senses we use to enjoy our various choices.

Want to do more?

Use the same procedure as above, only this time do one for "Things I Don't Care For." Make a class poster.

Language you can use

collage
art
favorite
food
family
friends
animals
toys
weather
choice

Things you will need

paste or glue

cardboard discs the size of a pizza wheel or large paper plates

assortment of magazines and catalogs

scissors
paper
pencil

Footprints Are Forever

Language you can use

finger
fingerprint
unique
updated birth certificate

The skin of the body extends over the entire outer portion of each person. In certain areas, the skin becomes very tough and develops in such a way that a design forms. Many of these skin designs can be found on the body, but the ones used specifically to identify each of us as special are the hands, fingers, and feet. The uniqueness of prints is such that criminals are identified by fingerprints and babies in hospitals are identified by footprints. Using this unique characteristic, let's celebrate birthdays by using them as an opportunity to thank parents.

Things you will need

letter quality typing paper

washable ink pad or finger paint

a sample birth certificate
a birthday child

What to do

1. Show the children a sample of birth records with foot or hand prints on them.
2. Discuss how these prints were made and why they were made. Every human being has a set of prints different from everyone else in the world. This shows the uniqueness of each person: "there is only one you."
3. What we would like to do is prepare a certificate on this special day for your parents to tell them how happy their special, unique child is to be a part of their family.
4. Make a certificate for the birthday child. Use the rhyme below or one of your own. Add foot and hand prints. Have children add their names. You may want to add other personal data such as height and age.

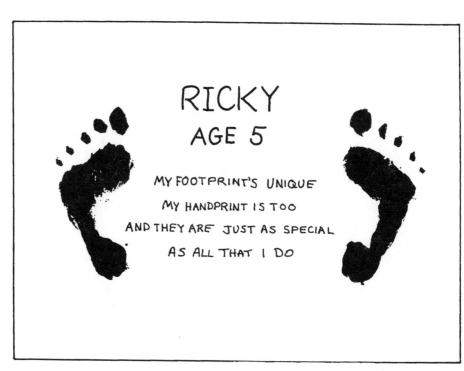

RICKY
AGE 5

MY FOOTPRINT'S UNIQUE
MY HANDPRINT IS TOO
AND THEY ARE JUST AS SPECIAL
AS ALL THAT I DO

Want to do more?

Make fingerprint pictures. Make a whole class hand and foot print mural. Have a police officer make fingerprints of the children for their parents.

An adult's skin covers about 20 square feet (two square meters). That is a rectangle one by two meters (three feet wide by six and a half feet long).

The outer layer of your skin is either dead or dying.

Color Me Special

Our skin color depends on how much pigment (coloring matter) we have in our skin. Everyone has some brown and yellow pigments in their skin. The amount of pigment we have depends on the amount our parents have. Since people have different amounts of pigments, there are many shades of skin color in this world of ours. Black children have lots of brown pigment and not much yellow in their skin. White children have a small amount of both yellow and brown in their skin. Asian children have more yellow and a small amount of brown pigment in their skin. Hispanic children will have more brown than yellow. Mixing pigments (colors) can be more than an art exercise. It can teach us about skin colors, how we are different, and how we are alike.

What to do

1. Introduce the word "pigment." Explain its meaning.
2. Let children mix colors individually and then make a painting of a face.
3. Compare the final paintings. Various shades should be evident.
4. Compare the shades of skin color to actual skin colors of children in the class or to photos if the class is not racially mixed.
5. This provides an excellent opportunity to discuss a world of differences.

Want to do more?

Discuss other racial characteristics such as hair and eyes.
If you have a lot of pigment (melanin) in scattered spots, you will have freckles. If you have melanin in large quantities all throughout your skin, then your skin is dark. How much melanin you have depends on how much melanin is in your parents' skin.

Language you can use

skin
color
pigment
brown
yellow
people
children

Things you will need

brown, yellow, and white tempera paint
brushes or Q-tips
paper

3+

Red, Brown, Blonde, Or Black, Kids Don't Have Grey Hair, That Is That

Language you can use

hair
colors
pigment
skin
texture
shape
count
observe
graph
curly
straight

Things you will need

large sheet of paper with a column for each hair color

black, brown, red, yellow, and white crayons

Our bodies are covered by skin. Hair is an outgrowth of the skin. The length of a hair depends on whether it is body, head, eyebrow, or eyelash hair. Hair grows until it reaches a certain length, then it falls out. When it falls out, a new one starts to grow in its place. Inside the hair is a pigment that gives the hair its color. When we grow older the pigment disappears and the hair becomes white. Hair can be coarse, fine, straight, or curly. It also comes in a variety of colors—black, brown, red, white, and blond. This activity uses graphing to indicate which and how many of these hair colors are present in your group.

What to do

1. Talk about hair. Talk about ways people change the look of their hair. We can make curly hair straight, straight hair curly, and even change our hair color. We can cut our hair or let it grow long. Have the children share their experiences and knowledge.
2. Ask the children to color in a square in the column that matches their hair color.
3. What is the most common hair color? If a column is empty, ask if anyone knows someone with that hair color.

Want to do more?

Graph curly and straight hair. Make hair color collages with magazine pictures. Make a separate one for each color. Use this as an opportunity to talk about similarities and differences among people.

Hair has a life span of two to four years.
The average head has 100,000 hairs.

Hair color determines the number of hairs per square inch. Blondes have more than redheads and more than brunettes, who have the smallest number.

Riddle me, riddle me, what is that,
Over the head, and under the hat? (hair)

A Very Hairy Collection

Most of the children have experienced head hair only through having it cut or washed. They have not looked at it closely or considered different types of hair. This classifying activity does that. The hair of the world can be classified into categories by color and texture. Hair texture is determined by the individual hairs, straight hair is round, curly or wavy hair is flat. This activity provides an opportunity to talk about differences in an interesting and positive way.

What to do

1. Talk with the children about different kinds of hair, the colors, the shades, the texture. Have pictures or samples of hair if your class has hair that is all about the same.
2. Make a collection of two or three hairs from each of the people in the room. Place each hair sample in a square, label it, and cover the posterboard with clear contact paper.
3. Cut the posterboard into individual hair cards. These can be sorted by color, length, and texture.

Want to do more?

Make a hair lotto board so the children can match hair to name. Visit a barber.

Hair that grows unevenly is curly. Straight hair is round, while curly hair tends to be flat.

Your hair grows two centimeters (three quarters of an inch) a month.

Hair grows faster during the daytime and in the summer.

Language you can use

hair
hair colors
(blonde, black, brown, grey, red)
hair texture
(straight, curly, wavy,)
bald

Things you will need

piece of posterboard with six centimeter (two inch) squares drawn on it—one for each child in the class

scissors
pen
clear contact paper

Long Hair, Short Hair, Everywhere

Language you can use

hair
grow
long
short
measure
follicle

Things you will need

pencil
thin strips of paper
marker

The only parts of the body that are hairless are the palms of the hands, soles of the feet, underside of the fingers, toes, and legs. Your hair is like a forest; some of the hair is old, some is young. Only when you examine hair closely do you see short and long hairs. Just how long is hair? Your children can measure their hair.

What to do

1. Talk about hair; explain that hair grows longer each day. Demonstrate how hair grows out of the skin. It grows out of places called follicles. This can be demonstrated by making a fist and pushing a pencil out through the fist. A hair starts growing and takes two to four years to grow. Everyone has hair.
2. On some places on our bodies the hair is shorter than others; some places have no hair. Can they find hair on their bodies? On the arms of young children hair is soft and fine, but it is there. Where does hair grow the longest?
3. The head is the place where hair grows the longest. We want to see where the longest hair on each child is found and measure that hair.
4. Measure everyone's hair. Use the strips of paper, tearing them off at the length of the longest hair. Write the child's name on the strip. Have the children predict whose hair is longest or shortest. What happens when you straighten out a curly hair?
5. Compare hair lengths using the strips. Were the predictions correct?

Want to do more?

Graph the results. Find adults with long hair and measure their hair. Visit a beauty or barber shop. Make a collection of hair for the class. Measure with a ruler how long the hair is in centimeters.

Hair is like a forest; each day new hair begins and old hair dies. In young children, the forest has many young hairs growing.

Hair can grow long. A man in India had hair that grew 8.5 meters (26 feet). Most people's hair never gets longer than three or four feet.

Simple Signs

Many people use their hands to talk to one another. This form of communication is called sign language. Many deaf people use sign language. Drivers, football players, baseball players, construction workers, traffic officers, and school crossing guards also communicate with signs. This activity focuses upon signs that the school crossing guard makes to both pedestrian and vehicle traffic. It introduces the children to the concept of non-verbal communication and provides a perfect lead-in for exploring sign language for the deaf.

What to do

1. Set up an intersection in the gym or on the playground. The intersection will have a crossing for the pedestrians. The traffic will be comprised of tricycles, wagons, and other wheel toys.
2. How can we get across this busy intersection? The traffic won't stop. We need a crossing guard or a traffic officer.
3. How does the crossing guard get the traffic to stop? She holds up her hands. Have children demonstrate how they have seen traffic halted. If they haven't seen this, ask them to invent a hand signal that they feel would stop traffic.
4. Practice hand signals that stop both people and traffic.
5. Now let's take turns being the crossing guard and directing both pedestrian and vehicle traffic by using our hands to communicate our commands.
6. Talk about other ways that hand-sign communication is used in activities such as baseball, construction work, or heavy duty equipment operations.

Want to do more?

Discuss sign language as used by deaf persons. Have a deaf person or teacher of the deaf visit your classroom and demonstrate some simple signs that the children can understand and use.

Language you can use

sign language
school crossing
traffic guard
direction
pedestrians
stop
go
sidewalk
street
intersection
vehicle
commands

Things you will need

wheel toys, for example, tricycle, wagon, scooter, etc

outdoor or indoor play space to accommodate wheel toys

Who Comes Out on Top?

Language you can use

trait
dominant
recessive
strong
weak
genetics

Things you will need

large sheet of paper and pen to record information

Each of us is a genetic map that represents parts of all those who are our ancestors. Each of us has traits that are passed down from parent to child. Some are found on both sides of the family. Some are passed down when the trait is seen in only one parent. When a trait shows itself over another through several generations, it is dominant. Brown hair and eyes are dominant traits. Blue eyes are recessive because that eye color will not generally exhibit itself if there is a brown-eyed parent. Recessive and dominant characteristics are important genetic knowledge. This activity offers an introduction to genetics by looking at the children's traits in a simple way. It also provides the opportunity to talk about differences among people in an interesting and positive way.

What to do

1. Ask the children to cross their fingers into the clasp position (see illustration).
2. Ask the children which thumb, the right or left, is on the top when they do this. Note who does what on a data table by name.
3. Cross arms. Which arm is on top? Record this information for each child.
4. Cross legs. Which leg is on top? Record the results.
5. Note on the data table which hand is dominant for each child.
6. Add up the numbers for each column. Which is on top most of the time?
7. Have the children "test" a parent or grandparent. Do they match or not?

Want to do more?

Graph the eye color of the children's pets. What is the most common eye color in animals?

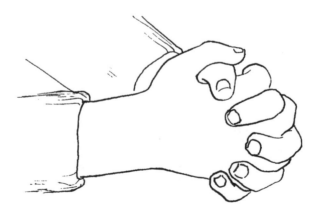

I N D E X